Sooner or Later

Personal Story Publishing Project Series

Bearing Up , 2018
- making do, bearing up, and overcoming adversity

Exploring , 2019
- discoveries, challenges, and adventures

That Southern Thing , 2020
- living, loving, laughing, loathing, leaving the South

Luck and Opportunity , sping 2021
- between if and if only

Trouble , fall 2021
- causing, avoiding, getting in, and getting out

Curious Stuff , spring 2022
- mementos, treasures, white elephants, and junk

Twists and Turns , fall 2022
- inflection points in life by choice, happenstance, misfortune, failure, and grace

Lost & Found , spring 2023
- loss and discovery—trials, serendipity, and life after

Available through Daniel Boone Footsteps
www.danielboonefootsteps.com
www.RandellJones.com
1959 N. Peace Haven Rd., #105
Winston-Salem, NC 27106

Sooner or Later

Randell Jones, editor

Daniel Boone Footsteps
Winston-Salem, North Carolina

Daniel Boone Footsteps
1959 N. Peace Haven Rd., #105
Winston-Salem, NC 27106

RandellJones.com
DanielBooneFootsteps.com
DBooneFootsteps@gmail.com

Cover image courtesy *123rf.com*
free images/bbtree

*Time is what keeps everything
from happening at once.*
– Ray Cummings
"The Girl in the Golden Atom"
All-Story Weekly, March 1919

Preface

This book is the ninth in a series of anthologies, collections of personal stories on a set theme, our Personal Story Publishing Project. Since beginning in 2018, our collections have included the themes: *Bearing Up*, "making do, bearing up, and overcoming adversity," *Exploring*, "discoveries, challenges, and adventure." *That Southern Thing*, "living, loving, laughing, loathing, leaving the South." *Luck and Opportunity*, "between if and if only" *Trouble*, "causing, avoiding, getting in, and getting out," *Curious Stuff*, "mementos, treasures, white elephants, and junk,." *Twists and Turns*, "inflection points in life by choice, happenstance, misfortune, failure, and grace," and *Lost & Found*, "loss and discovery—trials, serendipities, and life after."

The book you are holding is the result of our ninth Call for Personal Stories, this one on the theme: "Sooner or Later—time, timing, and inevitability." We thank the scores of writers who responded to the call by submitting such interesting, thoughtful, and well-crafted stories. They delivered the diversity and depth of perspective we were hoping for and the insight to self which proved we chose the right theme. Each story is about 750-800 words, so the writers were challenged in executing their craft, telling an interesting story succinctly. The writers and we have all found the Personal Story Publishing Project through its nine iterations, so far, to be an instructive and rewarding writing experience. For the readers, it is a delight.

We received submissions from many writers in North Carolina and across the South, notably, but also from writers reaching across the country from Florida, Pennsylvania, and New York to the West Coast. We wish we could have printed them all, but we are delighted to curate 50 stories for this collection.

In June 2019, we launched a second outlet for sharing these fine writers with a broader audience. Their work can now be heard in our twice weekly podcast, "6-minute Stories." Our podcast is available through Apple Podcasts (iTunes), Spotify, and Stitcher. You can listen directly to "6-minute Stories" and find all the stories archived at RandellJones.com/6minutestories. Episodes are announced on Facebook @6minutestories.

Sooner or Later, the Personal Story Publishing Project, and "6-minute Stories" podcast are undertaken by author and publisher Randell Jones, doing business as Daniel Boone Footsteps in Winston-Salem, North Carolina.

Thank you for enjoying and appreciating good storytelling. And, remember...

Everybody loves a good story.sm •

Contents

SOONER OR LATER

Contents

Contents

SOONER OR LATER

Contents

SOONER OR LATER

xvi

Introduction

S ooner or later, we will figure it out, we hope.

That phrase, "sooner or later," might make us think that whatever happens is inevitable, that it is only a matter of time, a plan, a calculation by forces of human nature or circumstances beyond our control that solves the equation for outcomes. Maybe.

Or perhaps we think that life is all a matter of timing, being in the right place at the right time with the right others, present or absent, that makes the difference, that teaches us how we come to think life works.

Or maybe "Sooner" and "Later" are just opposite sides on life's imagined timeline from wherever we find ourselves— or remember ourselves—one domain "before" and the other "after."

Maybe we are never exactly certain what is the right time or timing for whatever matters. Too much time, too little? Too soon? Too late? Or does time matter at all?

But sooner or later, we find out, we understand. We begin, we create, we finish, we love, we laugh, we cry, we cherish, we grieve, we rejoice, we learn. We take stock and we sort out the credit and the blame for life's experiences, tossing them into separate piles of pluses and minuses, satisfactions and regrets.

We are all pilgrims on separate paths which intertwine with the paths of others. We intermingle along the way, as distinct and separate as we think possible for us to be, only to discover that we all arrive at some same or similar eventuality, each with a different accounting along the way for how we got there, to that somewhere.

But sooner or later, we arrive, and we have our stories to tell. For that, we are grateful.

We are delighted by the response to our ninth Call for Personal Stories, and we are thankful to all the writers who invested time and energy into crafting personal stories for possible inclusion in this anthology. From among the submissions, we chose stories to include based on the quality of the writing and the resonance of the personal experiences shared with the announced theme, "Sooner or Later—personal stories about time, timing, and inevitability."

We have stories about the natural world and people in it, people cleansing their human spirit with a saddled-up ride through a forest, soaking up the natural world; the arrival of new species noted by their plumage, warbles, peeps, and chirps; and people unable to talk about changes in the earth's nature they can no longer ignore.

We have stories about people from afar and what that means at home: Amah, the village elder, offering hospitality and history, a different view of life and purpose and remembering. We have stories revealing that violence can be a part of life no matter where we live, and that to families of veterans still missing-in-action, being remembered is not the same as not being forgotten.

We have family stories showing that blood is thicker than water, that love can take a lifetime to come out, that sometimes the child must become the parent, and that holding hands can ease another soul across the final threshold.

One story makes a pitch for that family's generational love of baseball while another recounts those who begat us, while wondering how those rascals could possibly add up to us.

We read about the fear of inheriting the family curse, that one more try can ignite a life-saving spark, that grief is important in honoring someone you deeply love.

Stories reveal that making friends takes time; that in coupling, anticipation is a sign of deep affection, a respect for the laws of love and astronomical order; and that timeless love is expressed in five minutes of music.

For our self-discoveries, we have stories about teen lust and ancient poetry, reckoning with an undercurrent of wildness that interrupts life plans, the dire meaning of a clean desk, and living in synch from water to land and back again.

Once-treasured items are released to make new memories for new owners; good news nurtures our sense of aliveness, lifts our spirits, and heals; and living with the confidence of those who don't know a lot can be a dreadfully rude awakening.

Another story holds that we sometimes must pedal harder with danger only inches away as we stretch to do the extraordinary, while another suggests that sometimes satisfying our ambitions for how we want to see ourselves begins with comfortable shoes.

These are some of the stories among all those we share in this collection. We think our writers have brought their best for you to read and to consider. Whatever energy you bring to reading and rereading this collection, we hope you find these stories of time and timing having a positive influence in your life for the better—if not inevitably, then certainly sooner or later. •

RJ

Stir-fried Bee Chrysalis and the Soul Stories of Bright Beaded Hats

by Mary Alice Dixon

January 1986, Hani People Village
Yunnan Province, People's Republic of China

"She wants me to eat burnt worms?" I look at the government interpreter assigned to me.

"No," the interpreter, Chen, says. "Stir-fried bee chrysalis."

Sitting beside me on the wooden floor of the stilt house, a toothless Hani elder-woman hands me a bamboo bowl. She grins, motions for me to eat. Pigs scratch in the dirt below us. Their earthy smell permeates the house.

"Primitive." Chen shakes his head at the ways of the Indigenous People who live in this hill village between the Hong and Mekong Rivers.

A second interpreter directs my husband and our young son to another room.

Alone with Chen and the old woman, I take a bite of chrysalis, swallow cautiously, gratefully accept a cup of pu'er tea.

Back home in North Carolina, I am a teacher. Here among the Hani of Yunnan Province, I am a student. I want to learn how the Hani record history without a written language. Though I've picked up a few Chinese phrases since my family moved to another region of China the year before, those phrases don't help me here. The Hani speak a dialect of the Loloish language, not Chinese. I must rely on Chen, my handler, to translate.

"Call her Amah." Chen points to the elder-woman. "Grandmother."

"Thank you, Grandmother." I bow awkwardly as Chen translates. After another bite of stir-fried chrysalis, I ask, "Will Amah describe how the People remember their history, their stories?"

When she hears my question Amah's dark eyes shine. I wait.

Chen translates. "She says in the beginning the People journeyed to heaven seeking First Goddess's help. The People wanted to learn how to write words so they could keep their stories forever. First Goddess was wise. And sly. She knew written words do not keep forever. So, she gave the People written words, but she wrote them on ox hide."

Chen shakes his head. I say, "Ask Amah to continue."

"During the trip home the People got hungry. Very hungry." Chen frowns as he translates. "So, they ate the ox hide. Writing went inside them."

Amah touches my wrist, speaks.

"She says their language is in their bodies. To read like we do, she says, would make her People blind."

"Ask how they keep old stories alive."

Chen relays my question and Amah's answer. "Long ago a mother escaped a violent man by turning herself into a tree. The mother's son saw the tree, recognized his mother, carved the tree trunk, and freed her. Like bee from chrysalis. The story of the mother came out. Men carve wood to remember." Chen stands up. "Time to go."

"No, please. What about the women?" I point to Amah, then to myself.

Amah squats beside me, locks eyes with me. Then she reaches for a bamboo basket filled with multicolored cloth hats. She takes one out. The hat is covered with knotted strings, silver-colored coins, bright beads. She puts it on her head.

"Amah says the hat carries stories," Chen snorts. "Mother to daughter, many generations. Births, deaths. Stories in threads and beads." He snorts again. "Ridiculous. Native people must become modern."

"No, please." I touch a tangerine tassel on the hat. "What is the story of this?"

"Superstition," Chen answers.

A young man climbs the green bamboo ladder into the house. "Her grandson." Chen says.

Amah speaks to the young man. He speaks to me. To my surprise, he speaks English.

"Hats tell soul stories," the grandson says. "All people have twelve souls. You," he nods at me, "have twelve souls. Everybody knows, souls never die."

Chen looks at his watch. "No more fairy tales." Amah hands

Stir-fried Bee Chrysalis and the Soul Stories of Bright Beaded Hats the hat to me.

I hold it close, scribbling its details in my notebook. The hat has three silver-colored buttons, 12 embroidered zigzags, 50 yarn tassels, 64 embroidered squares, 68 silver-colored rondels, 89 white strings, and at least 1200 tiny tangerine, white, and turquoise-tinted beads. I am counting stories I am not given time to hear.

Then, despite my protests, Chen hustles me away. I rejoin my husband and son for the long bus ride back to our heavily monitored lodgings in Kunming City. The soul stories sewn in the hat remain in the village in the hills. Though the Cultural Revolution is over, I am in an era when it still casts long shadows.

But sooner or later, in the fullness of time, I believe one of my twelve souls will emerge from the chrysalis of my body and meet one of Amah's twelve souls. Then her soul will teach my soul the many stories that hat held. After all, as everybody knows, souls never die. •

Mary Alice Dixon is a Pushcart nominee who taught architectural history in the U.S. and China. She is an award-winning poet and finalist for the NC Poetry Society's 2023 Poet Laureate Award. Her writing appears in the PSPP anthologies *Twists and Turns*, *Curious Stuff*, *Trouble*, and *That Southern Thing*. She has recent work in *County Lines*, *Kakalak*, *Mythic Circle*, *Pinesong*, *Petigru Review*, and elsewhere. Mary Alice lives in Charlotte, NC where volunteers with hospice, participates in Charlotte Writers Club and Charlotte Lit, and loves hats, honeybees, and old stories.

The Origin of Lust
by Becky Gould Gibson

I didn't know the word "lust" when I was 10, but I sure as heck knew Elvis. "Love Me Tender," "Don't Be Cruel," "Hound Dog." I played 45's on the portable pink turntable my parents bought me for my birthday, danced with the door of the bedroom I had to share with my little brother Davey. Was that lust or its precursor? Proto-lust. Ur-lust, maybe. Fifth grade. I'd fallen for Johnny W___ in fourth, but never let him know it. "Liked" is how we put it. Johnny may have liked me too for a while, but he gave up for what he must've figured was my lack of interest. He took up with Betty Something-or-other who had breasts in sixth and in seventh crossed her legs in class and jounced her right leg over her left, while twisting a silver bracelet around one wrist.

If I had to guess when I started to feel lust, finally feel it, I'd say 10th grade. I was 14, going on 15. That's when breasts showed up. There they were, almost suddenly, the two of them. I slipped on the red cashmere pullover Mama had just bought me and checked myself out in the mirror. Turned to one side, then the other. My mother had no breasts to speak of, nor did my grandmothers. So, I was not looking for big. Just something. I stuck out my chest in that red sweater whenever I got the chance. Until then I'd worn mostly cardigans. Did Mama notice something I hadn't noticed?

I was filling out. Breasts, hips too. Well, what about that? Having breasts woke me up to my body. A little charge, a little excitement, kind of all over. Was that lust? Boys seemed irrelevant to what I was feeling.

Even then, I doubt I knew the word "lust." Most of what I'd gleaned so far about sex came from Ovid. In Latin. Little passages from *Metamorphoses* we translated for Elfrieda Cole's second-year class. Miss Cole never married. No "boyfriend" in sight. What was on her mind as Jove took one more nymph to the bushes? I never thought it odd she was having us read— not just read—but render, every delicious syllable, every ripe situation. I dutifully translated the passages she assigned us. I was beginning to get the picture.

The year before, I'd just moved to a new town, a new school. Scrawny, long-necked thing, tight pin curls, round-collared blouses. Shy, painfully shy. I'll never forget the day Miss Cole, a tidy woman in her fifties, introduced me to her first-year class. As I stood in front of the room, I could've sunk through the floor. Yet at her gentle urging, I was able to find voice enough to tell my classmates who I was and where I came from. Kind, yet rigorous, Elfrieda Cole was one of the best teachers I ever had. For the two years under her tutelage, I may have learned more about language and love than at any other time of my life. I'd signed up for Latin. Transformation is what I got. My career in lust—or trying to avoid it—had begun.

What intrigues me now on looking back is considering those stories from Miss Cole's perspective. What we called an "old maid" Latin teacher, opening the eyes of her nubile young charges not just to Latin, but to some of the hottest plots in Western literature. I entered her class with my nascent libido as yet untapped. What in the name of Jupiter was Miss Cole thinking—I mean, deep down—about Venus and Adonis or Pyramus and Thisbe or Echo and Narcissus or Daphne and Apollo? Yes, the passages came from a standard school text. But Elfrieda Cole was nothing if not thorough. My guess is she had the *Metamorphoses* well in hand while we were still in diapers. As she listened patiently to us read Ovid aloud in our halting English, I detected no hint of slyness in her expression. Had Elfrieda ever had a lover? Or was Ovid it?

The day I wore my new red cashmere sweater to class with my just-budded breasts, I felt—well, alive, in a way I'd never quite felt. My own breasts, not someone else's, no "light padding" to fill out the contours, as the bra-fitter at Ivey's counselled. (Frizzy red hair and ample bosom, which somehow made her an authority.) Advice of hers I did take: "Bend over, let your breasts fall into the cups." Precious little falling or filling. Still, they were there. It was during my sophomore year that the elements of lust came together. Red cashmere sweater. Breasts in evidence. Ovid chastely offered by Elfrieda. Boys, actual boys, would have to wait. •

Becky Gibson has published three chapbooks and five full-length books of poetry: notably, *Aphrodite's Daughter* (Texas Review Press,

The Origin of Lust

2007); *Need-Fire* (Bright Hill Press, 2007); *Heading Home* (Main Street Rag, 2014); and *Indelible* (The Broadkill River Press, 2018). Her current focus is creative nonfiction. Three pieces appear in print, in *Snowy Egret*, *Canary*, and *Twists and Turns* (PSPP, fall 2022). A fourth comes out soon in *Cold Mountain Review*.

Becky taught English at Guilford College until 2008, when she retired to write full-time. She lives in Chapel Hill, North Carolina.

Never Too Late To Say I Love You
by Mary Clements Fisher

Mama did not say I love you. Never, until near the end of her life, when she had less to lose.

A preschooler, I plinked on the piano in the upper register while Mama plunked out her choir pieces around middle C. I hummed the tunes with her until, under the spell of her singing, I slipped sideways into her pillowy lap. She stopped and stroked my cheek. No kiss. No words. Just the warmth and weight of her hand.

Music plucked a string in Mama's heart like words couldn't. When she signed me up for piano and voice lessons, I discovered a sure-fire way to gain her attention and affection. When I played or sang, her dimple surfaced in the sea of faces in the audience. As an adult, I questioned my people-pleasing nature, but as a kid, Mama's rare smile removed any doubt.

In my tweens, neither of us pleased the other. I unleashed my frustration in screeching "I hate you" episodes. How she remained unmoved baffled me. One afternoon, simmering in a pubescent sexuality soup, I accused her of never loving my father. After a sub-zero response, I slapped her.

Her face crumpled. Like a one-girl Greek chorus, I moaned my plea for her to hit me, please hit me, until hoarse. Brimming with sorrow, her steely eyes bored into my chest. She shut them. A tear trickled down her cheek. I couldn't face her anymore. Escaping into a field behind the house, I whacked dead cornstalks and collapsed sobbing. When I crept back into the kitchen, Mama pulled me into her arms, asked me to sit down, and shared memories of her childhood and marriage more painful than any punch—and more gutting than guilt.

Mama grew up in a household plagued with loss. Two baby sisters died before Mama turned 5, and her father forced her to kiss their cold lips goodbye. My grandmother grappled to cope with birth on birth, death on death, grief flooding the space where love once flowed. Years later, Grandma's surviving children nearly grown, Mama's favorite brother of three ended up in prison at 17. Another farewell. More mourning of a life ruined, youth lost to regrets, alcoholism, and premature death. Surviving six siblings, her father, her mother, and my father, Mama's mantra at each funeral expressed her lifelong anxiety. "Grief is what comes from getting attached." Even Mama's marriage devolved into a series of detachments.

Papa joined the Navy in 1941 and deployed for most of 13 years. When I turned 6, Papa returned home for good, and forever after, my parents slept in separate rooms. During junior high sleepovers, I breezed by this oddity and my friends' questions with a simple, "My dad snores." But Mama never said 'I love you' to him and shrank back when he bent to kiss her. Her coldness confounded me because his kindness and affection toward us 3 children soon made him beloved. But Mama never forgave him for loving his Navy career more than her, abandoning her to raise a teenage son and two young daughters alone. Loving her meant showing up.

When I visited my folks during college breaks, Mama clanged pots and pans in the morning to roust me out of bed. I caught on—she missed me. Showing up to share tea, toast, and chat bonded us over the years, but no words of love floated over our steaming cups. Her love notes arrived in her letters.

Until Alzheimer's silenced her, Mama wrote my siblings and me a letter every week, closing each with *Love, Mama*. No fear of immediate rejection. No physical demands. A distanced declaration. Did she write Papa letters those years he served overseas? Sign them *With* love? Did he write her back? After he died, she spoke of missing him, wrote tender poems about him, and recalled his smile when she stroked his brow as he lay dying. She'd re-attached to Papa after 25 years of aging and sharing tea and toast with him. Widowed, she changed.

When I arrived on her doorstep during her last decades, she still didn't kiss me. I hugged her, kissed her weathered cheeks, and played the piano and sang for her whenever she asked. But each time I climbed into my car to leave, she embraced me and murmured "I love you, Mary."

"Love you too, Mama. Always." Her dimple buried in deep wrinkles matched mine. Her bent body, arms outstretched waving goodbye, melted in the rearview mirror in my blur of tears. •

Never Too Late To Say I Love You

Mary Clements Fisher celebrates her current mother/grandmother, sweetheart, student, and writer status in Northern California. Her poetry and prose explore her mad, muddled, and magical moments. She's published in *Quail Belle Magazine, Adanna Journal, Passager Journal, The Weekly Avocet,* Personal Story Publishing Project, *Prometheus Dreaming Journal, The Closed Eye Open, Capsule Stories,* and *They Call Us Magazine.* Join her @maryfisherwrites and https://maryfisherwrites.squarespace.com/

Ten Places I Have Lived with Violence

by Wanda Freeman

1961,
Enid, Oklahoma

A half-duplex next to a tree-lined alley, where a boy in a red jacket paced the sidewalk as I roller skated until just the right moment, when he grabbed my arm and dragged me scraping and screaming and didn't let go until the babysitter stuck her head out the door.

1967, Harvey, Louisiana

The house with peeling paint and beadboard walls, next door to the landlord's nice brick home, where I sassed Grandpa and he stepped over the puppy guard, chased me to the last room, and yanked at the corded phone I gripped; where I swatted his hand, and he swung for a slap and scratched my lip; where I called my mother and she called my uncle, who came over, outraged, and scolded me for hitting the old man.

1973, Gretna, Louisiana

A single-wide in a graveled row of trailers and troubles, where my boyfriend discovered I really was a virgin; where I had a pregnancy scare, checked myself in the bathroom and murmured, "Oh, Mama, I'm pregnant"; where he fell to his knees sobbing when I suggested we break up.

Ten Places I Have Lived with Violence

1974, Algiers Point, New Orleans
The apartment made of two giant parlors in a Greek Revival, where one Mardi Gras evening, my boyfriend's sister shoved her glass-domed anniversary clock from the mantel to the unforgiving floor after her husband second-lined up Bourbon Street with a woman dressed as a French maid; where I threw an ashtray that skidded unbroken across both parlors, certain my boyfriend still loved that girl he always talked about.

1977, Algiers Point, New Orleans
The T-shaped one-story, a multicolored maze inside, where he became another person and slammed me to the floor, one, two, three times before I escaped, slept in a hotel, and returned to roses and remorse; where I lay trembling beside him and dreamed that I turned away from a monster's flaming tower, and where I told him he could never touch me like that again or I'd leave.

1978, New Orleans
Our 1960s brick ranch, where hope fought for life and one of everything grew in the backyard; where during our nightmarish last year he threatened to hit me, jeering that it wasn't the same as actually hitting me; where he jabbed his wrist with a fork during dinner, tested a cord he had slung around a tree limb, and finally shot himself in our living room; where I let my mother visit post-funeral and she recalled once dreaming that she heard me cry, "Oh, Mama, I'm pregnant."

1993, Canton, Michigan
A small, white-walled apartment in a big noisy complex, where my husband proposed as I lay tranquil beside him; where the

couple next door often blasted the stereo like a heavy-metal concert, the woman later emerging with her bangs drawn, a failed curtain over throbbing black eyes.

1998, Ypsilanti, Michigan
The upstairs apartment carved from an off-campus house, where police came twice in one week to check me for bruises before we figured out the nightly quarrels were coming from the drama students downstairs rehearsing *Who's Afraid of Virginia Woolf?*; where on a late-summer night extended shouting brought long guns and flashing lights to the blue house two doors down, and the man they took away in handcuffs hollered, "You broke my heart, Loretta!"

2017, College Hill, Greensboro, North Carolina
The perfect condo in an imperfect world, where a hundred feet from our door a couple were mugged at gunpoint; where one Halloween, eight shots were fired and a car screeched past, jumped a curb, sideswiped a light pole, thunked the basement of a corner house, and squealed away; where the following midnight a parade of motorcycles and black SUVs rumbled up to mark their turf; where a brawling couple brought their war to our doorstep in a rusty van, he hopped out, and she shattered his windshield with a bat; where we considered getting a gun or a dog and settled on zapper walking sticks; where mere days before we moved, twin shots from two speeding cars ricocheted into a bedroom in the building next door.

2022, Greensboro, North Carolina
The suburban-looking home on a suburban-looking street

Ten Places I Have Lived with Violence

where we lost the habit of locking our cars until thieves rifled through our consoles and stole our allergy pills. "I feel violated," my husband said. "Me too," I said. Where we unpacked our zapper sticks and leaned them by the door. •

Wanda Freeman lives in Greensboro, North Carolina. She is an award-winning writer, editor, and journalist whose literary work has appeared in *The MacGuffin* (Schoolcraft College, Livonia, Michigan) and *Cellar Roots* (Eastern Michigan University, Ypsilanti). She grew up in New Orleans, where she learned to cook and second-line. She holds a bachelor's degree in English literature from the University of New Orleans and a master's degree in creative writing from EMU. She is a member of the North Carolina Writers' Network and enjoys performing her work at open mic events.

Andante con Amore

by Rhoda Cerny

Five decades ago, doctors advised my mother, a recently wedded young musician, against pregnancy. Inflammation from cancer was taking over her body and she did not have much time to live. I am grateful she ignored them.

What kind of woman attempts to get pregnant on her deathbed?

A brave one. A woman who does her research and knows the hormones might help to battle her disease and extend her time; a woman whose career as an internationally recognized violist gives her a life filled with music and travel and a longing to extend it; a woman in love with her husband of only one year who wants to give him a child as a reason to carry on; a woman who wants to leave something of herself behind so she is not forgotten; a woman who wants to experience the motherly bond before exiting this world; a woman who believes any offspring of hers will survive and thrive, even after she is gone.

I am that last-minute child: a product of love, a burst of life, a last chance gift.

We gave each other time. We shared three whole years: hiking together in the mountains of Western North Carolina, me tied to her back; picnicking on the Blue Ridge Parkway; dancing to Nana Mouskouri's *"Soleil, Soleil"* over and over; playing with the tiny brown teddy bear attached by a keychain to the rosin in her viola case. My last memory of her is from my third birthday party—her red wooden sandals, red and white-checkered apron, and matching towel.

I am now eleven years older than my mother ever was. When I study her photos, it seems like she could be my younger sister. Will a time come when she will look as though she could have been my child?

What is time but imagination?

I still imagine her as older than me, the same age as her best friend, Miwako, a violinist whose daughter, Maika, I envy for growing up in the classical music world, for being a leader in her field, for having a husband and children, and, most of all, for having a mother to witness it.

Hailing from opposite coasts, Maika and I shared our lives in letters. At 18 years old, I left Boone, North Carolina, and journeyed by train to Los Angeles where we met for the first time. Her family greeted me at the station with a handful of balloons. They knew I loved zoos, so we went to all of them. We took a trip to Mexico to see the wild horses on the beach and attended Maika's piano recital.

Best of all, I met "my mother." Being around Miwako felt like being around my mom. I reveled in her stories of their time together as budding musicians: train trips across Europe; elegant dresses; concert hall performances; master classes with Pablo Casals; recording music; cocktail parties and dating; busking on cobblestoned streets. Through the photos she shared I envisioned my mother's life and what it was like to know her.

Years later, I moved to Los Angeles to study acting. I attended Maika's wedding on a cliff overlooking the ocean in Palos Verdes Estates. They said their vows under a trellis covered with white flowers, on a green lawn shaded by palms, water glistening in the sun beyond. Members of the Los Angeles Philharmonic, Miwako's friends, performed. One played Bach on a handsaw with a violin bow. Friends and family shared their stories about the bride and groom, reliving how they met, performing a piano duet in college. Always near her daughter, Miwako's proud laughter brightened the room.

Might this be my life if my mother had lived?

Recently I paused in the hallway in front of a childhood photo of my mother and me laughing together. Inspired, I located the CD that one of her colleagues had made from her recording of Schumann, Stamitz, and Vaughan Williams. I listened to her voice in the sound of her viola d'amore. I found her vintage evening dresses tucked in a corner of my closet and tried them on, imagining the concerts where they were first worn. A wooden decoupage jewelry box made in

Europe with her black and white photo inside the lid still holds a treasure of silver jewelry from around the world, including a charm bracelet representing each country of her travels. Her viola was sold after she died and though I long to see the tiny teddy bear that was lost to mildew, I revive my memories as a 3-year-old by singing "*Soleil, Soleil*" to my cats, Figaro and Aria. I try to imagine what motherhood is like, and I wonder what it must have meant those many years ago to my mother, Rhoda Lee.

Con amore. •

Rhoda Cerny lives in Chapel Hill, North Carolina, with her two cats. When she is not writing or dreaming of travel, you will find her singing, dancing, practicing Italian, and gardening. A member of the Orange County chapter of the NC Writer's Network and writing groups in the Triangle, she has published poetry and is currently working on a novel and a memoir. She wrote "*Andante con Amore*" while a Writer-in-Residence at the Weymouth Center for the Arts and Humanities in Southern Pines.

Bonds

by Annette L. Brown

Crack! The bat-to-ball contact shoots 43,000 fans from their seats. Between our claps and shouts, my son asserts, "Mom, we're watching history! This is history!" He bounces on the balls of his feet. His teen eyes reflect the sparkle of stadium lights and child wonder, dazzled by the moment. We're in San Francisco, August 8, 2007, the Giants vs. the Nationals, bottom of the fifth inning. Barry Bonds has just hit his 756th career home run, breaking Hank Aaron's 33-year record. Fireworks rain over the bay. The crowd roars. Swept up by the scope of the accomplishment and the joy of witnessing it, I bounce in rhythm with my son.

As Bonds jogs the bases, a movie reel of personal memories makes that slow trek with him, frames connected in curled ribbons. For all my life, baseball has decorated my family's spring and summer like a seasonal centerpiece.

My father raised me on orange-and-black. As a toddler, I nestled in the pocket of his crossed legs, eating deviled egg sandwiches and listening to the game on his portable transistor radio. My dad whooped, so I whooped. We shouted in concert

whenever the Giants turned two, hit a blooper or a bomb.
I was always Team Dad.

As Bonds finishes circling the bases, Willie Mays comes onto
the field to join his godson in celebration. My dad loves Willie
Mays, so I love Willie Mays. For years, talk of the *Say-Hey* Kid
spiced our dinner conversations. We followed his career,
marveled at his athletic feats, even huddled in front of the TV
for his last at-bat. Leaning forward, elbows on knees, we
settled in the twin sags of our two-cushion couch for the 1973
World Series. Indifferent to Mays being a New York Met at the
time, we cheered the man. We wished Mays success—a home
run, even a dinger or flare, something to get him on base.
We hoped he'd go out a hero. He didn't—he grounded into a
fielder's choice. Flattening into the couch back as if the air had
been let out of him, my dad rested his hand on my shoulder,
his eyes still focused on the screen. It was a quiet goodbye
to our favorite player.

The applause subsides in AT&T Park. Hank Aaron appears
on the jumbotron to relinquish his record and congratulate
Bonds. Older now, the face filling the screen still resembles the
athlete I applauded at Candlestick Park in 1974, not long after
his push past Babe Ruth's home-run record. Game over, my
brother and I, hoping to spy our heroes, gripped the chain
links of the players' parking lot fence. Eyes wide, we watched
Aaron leave the locker room sandwiched between four armed
guards, their rifles pressed to their chests. A clump of coordi-
nated steps, the group resembled an awkward crab as they
crossed the 30-foot stretch of asphalt to the open doors
of the team bus.

I did not know Aaron had received hundreds of death threats—a situation so serious it warranted guards with guns. I didn't realize a Black man breaking a white man's record could lead to such an extreme response. However, at 14-years-old, I did recognize the wrongness of what I was witnessing. I stared unblinking—heart racing, fingers of one hand tightening on the fence, the other reaching for my brother. The guns did not bother me. I grew up in a family of hunters. But guns needed to protect a player did.

Fans are quick to romanticize baseball. I do it—the diving catches, the monster home runs, the rookie batter fending off 12 pitches against the veteran on the mound. The battles are heroic. But that day as I watched Aaron escorted to his bus, no heroism or romance was in play. Instead, the ugly side of humanity burned that image into my memory.

Sparks, like fireflies, hang lonely in the distance. Mays and Aaron grace the field and screen—heroes I shared with my father and now with my son, whose experience of this moment is untainted by musings over the fact that racism and other human failings are sometimes players. Another day I may tell him about the time I saw guns in baseball, but not today. He has a lifetime to learn. We will let this day be about celebrating a lifetime achievement.

I turn from the field to watch my son, who wears a full-face smile, freckles scattered over flushed cheeks, breaths woven with awe. His joy warms me. Being a fan encourages us to make space for hope—the promise of the next pitch, the next at-bat, the next game, the happy ending. •

Bonds

Annette L. Brown is a mother, wife, and retired teacher, who lives on an almond farm in Central California where she enjoys spending time with family and friends. She is grateful for the support of The Taste Life Twice Writers and The Light Makers' Society and for simply having time to write. Annette has pieces reflecting her love of nature, family, beauty, and humor in several publications including *Cathexis Northwest Press, Last Stanza Poetry, Flash Fiction Magazine, Every Day Fiction,* and other Personal Story Publishing Project anthologies.

Five Minutes More

by Diana Neunkirchner

The other two girls in our band counted out tips in the smoky barroom. "Only twelve bucks? Bummer."

It didn't feel that way to me. We were getting better—our harmonies and riffs were spot on. But when we split up, my solo act fell flat. Like them, I thought I'd feel better making money.

My mother offered her advice, "Marry a good breadwinner so you can loaf around." Before she met my father, she was a concert violinist and played for love, not money. She stopped after my brother was born. No more time for music.

In a twist of fate, I met my forever man at a speakeasy. This handsome man with a jovial smile and ocean blue eyes captured my heart with his road stories. That summer, he persuaded me to come with him to California. So, I traded my guitar for love and adventure—a five-minute decision that changed everything.

Out West, time is a fast-paced freeway. I paid the tolls with a straight face and calloused hands. After two years of real work and sacrifice, my husband completed his internship, and we were expecting our first child. I did not realize it then, but I needed love to make music again, and more time.

"There's a swap meet Saturday," he suggested. "Let's go. We might get lucky." We emptied our cookie jar, picked coins from the roadster's ashtray, and sold our two guinea pigs—small sacrifices, but they added up. He stuffed our $15 of hope in his wallet.

We wandered through the open market, a repurposed drive-in outside of Beverly Hills. After a few hours, we were hungry and I had not packed lunch. I feared we'd soon be eating my guitar money.

Faint music drifted through the rows of vendors. *A woodwind? Flute?* I grabbed his hand. "Let's find that sound." We skipped together, my hero whistling Jethro Tull's "Nothing Is Easy." I felt a surge of energy.

We found the music maker, a thin girl playing an unusual flute. At her booth, dozens of ceramic instruments, each a work of exquisite beauty, lay exposed in their open cases. While a small crowd encircled her wares, she continued playing, the perfect sales pitch.

On impulse, I picked up a porcelain tube glazed in midnight blue. My fingers fell perfectly on the holes. Before I could form the embouchure, I locked eyes with the merchant who had stopped playing.

"Ten dollars. Includes the book," she proclaimed.

Without reservation, my music-lover gave Janis Joplin's look-alike the money. He winked at me saying, "Darling, promise you'll play it at least five minutes every day."

My promise became a habit. For five minutes a day, I played for love.

Years later during a Vermont winter, our first born accidentally bumped the table where my perfect pastime rested. It rolled off, shattering into countless shards.

"Write to the flute maker," my husband urged. "Maybe they can help."

In early December, I stuffed my sadness into an envelope addressed to the Reliable Brothers Flute Company. I was fluteless for months. When Spring came with tulips and snow drops, I became desperate for merry making, my habit waning like the moon.

In June, the handsome man with ocean blue eyes handed me a package, and not a minute too soon. "This came for you a few days ago, but we saved it for your birthday." He kissed me, light and sweet.

Our little girls giggled. "Can you play Happy Birthday, Mommy?" Five minutes split into octave scales and funny songs.

We were a family of six when we moved to North Carolina. With help from friends, we restored an old farmhouse, fully embracing our country life. When sleep stalled on our

homestead, I'd play lullabies to soothe my restless audience.
But when kids grow up, they find their own music. Old
lullabies stay behind.

And when spouses pass away, lullabies become laments. In five
minutes a day, with lungs full of grief, I played them all.
I wondered if I'd ever feel love blowing through my
instrument again.

Recently, I hiked along the Eno River with friends. While we
whistled with the mockingbirds, I heard music from porcelain
tubes of midnight blue and shared my flute stories with them.

"Oh, I have a flute like that," one hiker declared. "I got it for
my husband, but he never played it." Our stories entwined like
dancing angels, each part fulfilling the whole. A week later, she
sold me that flute for a C-note—thank you—on what would
have been the 70th birthday of the handsome man with a
jovial smile.

I kept my promise that night playing five minutes more
for love. •

Copyright 2023, Diana Neunkirchner

Diana Neunkirchner is a retired teacher living in Rougemont, North
Carolina. An avid reader and writer, she is a member of the Durham
Writers Group, the Writers Inspirational Network, and the Writers
Critique Group. When she's not writing short stories, personal
essays, or memoir, she is hiking along the Eno River or playing the
flute at Your Saving Grace, the family farm.

Awakened in Rome
by Okira Odani

I am a Japanese American, born and raised in Tokyo, who moved to the United States in my early twenties. I became bilingual through dedicated study as a teenager and then more fluent and bicultural through an excellent education at Brown University graduate school. The skill, rare at the time, of bridging the language and culture gap between these two vastly different world economic powers allowed me to work as a professional interpreter. Indeed, I served over years as a simultaneous interpreter for countless business leaders and two U.S. Presidents. But after about 15 years of traveling the world in that occupation, an ordinary scene I encountered by chance in Rome awakened me to awareness of another cultural difference, one that persuaded me to shift how I viewed my life.

In the early evening after an assignment, loosening my necktie and flinging my suit jacket on my shoulder, I strolled back to my hotel through a deep-green cypress and pine-lined street where restaurants and boutiques lured tourists. I had performed my duty well that day. My heart was light with a sense of accomplishment. The setting sun shone gold on ancient earth-colored ruins nearby, brightening the building façade, store awnings, and caned chairs fronting the cafes.

On the way, a burst of laughter and the joyful cries of children caught my attention. I stopped and looked into a shaded alley. An older man, bald and red-faced, in his undershirt, sweaty and tattered, grinning mischievously, ran around in his sandals, kicking a soccer ball with several youngsters, possibly his grandchildren. The playful scene radiated genuine happiness. The aroma of home cooking, tomato sauce, roasted garlic, and baking bread wafted in the air, waiting for the players to come in for the family supper.

Inexplicably and suddenly, the scene pierced my heart with chilling sadness. I had not seen my children in New York for almost ten days. Minoru, my shy twelve-year-old, had begun junior high school that September. I wondered if he could manage his new curriculum. My 3-year-old, lively and curious Shigeru, might ask where his father was. Until that moment on the street, I had been content with the glamour of traveling and working for the leaders of governments and corporations. I was proud that I had a particular skill. The job paid well; it enabled me to fulfill my fatherly obligations.

I had grown up in a Tokyo household where my father was absent, allegedly due to his work schedule. I thought that was normal, and I do not have memories of missing him. In the male-dominated society of traditional Japan, a man's place was outside the home. My mother complained about his not coming home some nights, but she did not expect him always to be around.

My wife was also from Japan, and it did not occur to me that my family could miss me at home. During the peak of my interpreter's career, I traveled constantly, sleeping in hotel rooms in far-away cities for over 200 days of the year. That was a sign of success as far as my ego was concerned—I met the needs of world leaders. My self-esteem stayed high and blinded me to my family's needs.

In Rome, I awoke to the surprising reality that I missed my children. I wanted to hear their voices, chuckles, and their stories of the day, even by telephone. I called New York, self-obsessed and forgetting the time difference. My wife answered the phone. "No, they are not here. They are at school." I did not detect in her voice her missing me, although I deserved it. I did not say that I missed her. Nothing was unusual for her husband to be absent from home. The tradition we both grew up with worked against my right to feel homesick.

I did not have much appetite for dinner that evening. Instead, I descended to the bar in the hotel's basement and ordered some stiff drinks. Alcohol numbed my senses but not the loneliness, the chilly, empty soul. *I may be at the end of this career.* I thought. *My job no longer feels as satisfying as it felt moments ago. Do my boys miss me? I want to play with them ... with a soccer ball. I must fly home to my children*, I decided. I did.

With its rich history and philosophy about crucial matters of the heart, the ancient city of Rome conspired to grant me a moment to reflect on my hectic life. Providing financially

for my family and polishing my ego proved to be lacking.
I discovered that what I really wanted was the intimacy of love
the old man and his tiny companions showed me that night on
the streets of Rome as the sun was setting on the day and they
prepared for eating their evening meal together as a family. •

Akira Odani lives in the ancient city of St. Augustine, Florida.
He belongs to Taste Life Twice Writers and the Florida Writers
Association. Born in Tokyo, he had written extensively for the
Japanese media. Still, more recently, his interest has turned to writing
in English and subjects related to his experiences interacting with the
two cultures. Some of his work has appeared in the pages of FWA
anthologies, *The Weekly Avocet*, PSPP's *Twists and Turns* and *Lost &
Found*. He stays active, meditating, swimming, and playing pickleball.

More To Live For

by Robin Russell Gaiser

1968

April

Martin Luther King, Jr has been shot to death. I am getting married in three weeks. My wedding dress, my mother's ivory slipper satin gown, which she wore in 1945 to wed my father after the War, is being altered in the bridal salon at Woodward and Lothrop in downtown Washington, D.C.

But Washington is burning.

Dark, rancid smoke hangs over my parents' house in Alexandria, Virginia, six miles away. I have driven home from the College of William and Mary where I am a senior, to have the final fitting.

King is dead and I'm worrying about a wedding dress. Henry, my blue-eyed, muscled husband-to-be, a newly commissioned Marine officer, has orders to Vietnam six weeks after our dress-white military wedding. "I want to get married before I go," he says at Christmas. "More to live for."

My mother and I brave I-95, plead our case to the armed National Guardsman who stops our car. He waves us around the barricade. "Be careful. Lucky for you, Woodward and Lothrop is safe right now."

June

Robert Francis Kennedy is gunned down in Los Angeles. Henry and I have flown to Southern California after our wedding and my final exams. We bunk on base at Camp Pendleton as he prepares to ship out. But today we are in Los Angeles. We reserved tickets for Disneyland. Our radio alarm wakes us in our hotel with the news that RFK has been shot. Will Disney be open? Should we go?

We need Disneyland. Please give us this tinseled-up, make-you-laugh-and-forget day. Please transport us out of this world. Maybe Bobby will make it, we tell ourselves. We shower, dress, eat breakfast, our transistor radio plastered to Henry's ear. We drive to Disneyland. People wander around. The sky is gray.

Bobby Kennedy dies. The music, the rides, the manufactured fun shut down, then start right up again. Is it moments or minutes we stood frozen, heads down.

We stay at the park, but I hardly remember. We hold hands and meander. Even Disney can't manufacture fun. Young, in love, newly married. And our lives in a war zone.

July

Henry Alverson Ledford is killed in action. Shot to death point blank by Viet Cong. Soggy, vicious Vietnam. He was brave, unafraid, tough, manly in this world. He thought he had to go. And I think I must be a brave, unafraid, tough widow. Friends march against the war. How can I?

After Henry's full-military-honors funeral at Arlington, I live with my parents. I cannot sleep; still hear the cadence of the drums, see his flag-draped casket, the riderless horse; feel my fury toward tourists filming our entourage snaking up the hill to his gravesite. My teaching job begins in five weeks. I have missed my graduation.

My wedding dress hangs shrouded in blue plastic.

August
I buy a light blue sports car. Top down, I roar at 114 mph on the Dulles Toll Road. No one hears me scream over the blaring radio. It is midnight.

I move into an apartment with a college girlfriend before school starts. We both begin teaching. My five classes of American Lit. total 175 students. A few boys are close to my age. They often stare. I sponsor four new clubs, attend all sports events, ride the raucous pep club bus. At night I am plagued with violent nightmares.

My principal sends me a note during first period: "You do not have to attend the U.S. Marine Corps Band assembly today. Your classes are covered." I go anyway; sit in the back; leave midway.

1969
July
Gordon holds me as I wail against his bare chest on our honeymoon. We are in Ireland. One year ago on this day, Henry was killed in Vietnam. Tall, muscular, blue-eyed Gordon and I, teachers at the same school, kept our romance secret

until I showed up with an engagement ring on April Fools' Day. No one believed us.

I dread his two-week Navy reserve training duty in Tampa, Florida. We kiss. Say good-bye. Then he drives away.

1971
May
I teach English: poetry, critical reading and writing, mass communication. I have co-authored the curriculum. Gordon completes an MA at Georgetown, secures a job for the fall. We buy an older house in Falls Church, move in, walk the neighborhood and relish the tree cover, rhododendron, and azaleas. I garden, decorate. He repairs and paints.

My doctor calls at school. Top down on my little blue sports car, I sing for joy all the way home at a cautious 35 mph. We are expecting a baby. •

Robin Russell Gaiser, MA, CMP, holds degrees in English literature and psychology and a certificate in therapeutic music. She has published two books, *Musical Morphine: Transforming Pain One Note at a Time* (Pisgah Press: 2016) and *Open for Lunch* (Pisgah Press: 2018) and numerous short stories, poetry, and narrative non-fiction. She is a vocalist and multi-instrumentalist as well as creator of Appalachian folk art. Her three children and their spouses, plus five grandchildren live coast to coast. She and her husband, Gordon, live in Asheville, North Carolina. www.robingaiser.com

In Time a Reckoning
by Thomas Gery

My life's journey before and after the Peace Corp reflected the opening lines to Charles Dickens' *A Tale of Two Cities:* "It was the best of times, it was the worst of times ...." And in time there would be a reckoning.

I did much by age 25: college, war and back, the work world, a return to the campus. With sheepskin in hand, and a steamer trunk of experiences the next stop was social services. I took a position at a prestigious institution as part of a youthful cadre of counselors helping kids. It was the best of times.

I wore the uniform of respectability, a role model for youth. Yet underneath was something unsettling. My baggage included the horror house of a combat zone where convention is upended. Rules of engagement contradict religious commandments. A dead military age male in a free-fire zone was a number to be counted. Enthusiastically following orders can lead to moral injury. I brought trouble home with me.

I gained confidence to maintain the decorum of a wise counselor. Our young group worked well together, often meeting for conferences, case reviews, cafeteria lunches.

We became close as staff; I and another went further.
My after-hours self included an undercurrent of wildness.

I was single with no one special; she was in an open marriage.
We were colleagues collaborating on cases, in her office or
mine. It led to quiet, evening rendezvous. Clandestine liaisons,
wine, weed, heady discussions and physical desires all blended
into a torrid affair. I also felt free to roam, moral compass
spinning wildly. I was on the prowl heading toward the worst
of times.

I weighed the options. We understood the romantic entan-
glement pointed to a dead end. She was not free,
nor I committed. Heartfelt notes were anonymous.
Each was satisfied for different reasons. We parted warmly;
her final missive, "… Love and take care—Me."

Other aspects of my life flashed red warnings. Too much
carousing, being stoned at the wrong times, conflicted with the
new work life. I needed a change, something akin to running
away. The Peace Corp offered a time out, a virtuous alternative.

I calculated that time away in a foreign country held promise.
The Peace Corp required two years—a reasonable commitment
for a 20-something. I buttressed my decision with the rationale
that surviving Vietnam proved anything less was easy and
I would save money for a career-building graduate degree.

A Peace Corp volunteer lives with hardship, sacrifice, and
challenges requiring steadfast resolve. During the initial weeks
of orientation, I began to rethink my decision; escape was not

a sound *raison d'être*. I suffered physical malaise caused by accli-mation to equatorial Africa. Years later Plasmodium vivax, malaria, put me in hospital. Mentally, I took a hit by relocating to the underdeveloped world. Within two months I was back in the USA.

I had made a huge mistake. The sting of misadventure caused me to feel diminished in the eyes of my friends. I imagined a scarlet "L" branded on my forehead—*Loser!* Reality reinforced the loss of face. I had gone from independent, young profes-sional to unemployed failure living in the parental basement. Shame and guilt brought the worst of times. It felt like a reckoning.

My life's journey had been following a destructive path. I boldly forced a course correction by entering the Peace Corp. I suffered unintended consequences—regret and self-reproach for quitting. And the deep-seated source of my alienation, memories of war, remained, as did the self-medicating. Years became decades with the memories on lock-down, the habits barely under control, the uniform of respectability worn only with effort.

As the COVID pandemic stalked the world in 2020, I took steps to again change course. I did a moral inventory. Unbridled enthusiasm in a combat zone is injurious; equating body counts to scoring touchdowns dehumanizing. Addiction serves to bandage a festering wound. With the passing of time, I had a complete reckoning. Recovery is healing.

I found the best of times. •

In Time a Reckoning

Thomas Gery, a common man with uncommon experiences lives in Berks County, Pennsylvania. He served in the U.S. Army with duty in Vietnam. As a social worker he helped children, youth, and adults in a variety of practice venues and situations throughout a work life of 40 years. Married with two adult children and two grandchildren, he is currently writing his life's story to provide answers to questions his kids will never ask. His first essay appeared in Personal Story Publishing Project—*Lost & Found*, 2023.

Blueberries and Nubians

by Bill Donohue

I began my Saturday with a self-wallowing sense of indecision. The previous evening I'd endured an after-hours brain MRI at an imaging center with dissonant, jarring noises and both the machine's discomfort and the recognition that my lung cancer diagnosis needed the clarity of location. More importantly, we prayed this brain image hopefully would rule out any evidence of presence or spreading there.

On the way home we wandered through a darkened neighborhood with the help of GPS and growing hunger to find the annual Winston Salem Greek Festival. Music and joyous dancing seemed to encircle us as we neared the large tent and smells of spanakopita and moussaka wafted across the parking lot for our drive through meals. It was a welcome bump in the disquieted attitude I harbored.

On my mind this morning and lingering from the previous evening was my daughter's admonition to put aside my too-consuming discouragement and disgust with the North Carolina General Assembly, parallel national concerns and think positively about the many good things in my life and in the world. She was in the best possible position to offer that,

Blueberries and Nubians

having just announced from her home in Norway that my second grandchild was now the size of a blueberry, and I was the first to know about it!

She was offering me an attitudinal option to start my weekend. The medical diagnosis would have more clarity eventually and I could then decide just how I was going to fight it. In the meantime, my mind and heart were opening to the more positive aspects of my life.

I'd been encouraged earlier in the week by a friend in Wilmington, hours away, to visit the Winston Salem Fairground Farmer's Market and visit a "Juice Jumper." This lady would offer me an on-the-spot seminar on all things good about kale and juice cocktails. Open to the clear option of nutritional power-partnering with my cancer care team, what could I lose?

The first booth I visited, like most I scanned down the barn-filled array of vegetables, fruits, and sun-weathered farmers found a black man stirring sausage and chopped vegetables for sample cups, to which he nodded my ascent. His eyes lit up and he said, "I know you from somewhere!" Within moments we connected and recounted his days as a photographer for the Department of Parks and Recreation and an iconic photo he took of my son and me in Special Olympic Partner Golf competition. He smiled with pride as we walked through the many publications that enjoyed many more than a thousand words with that photo and adorned my kitchen wall. It began a small world realization that sooner or later all our lives connect. He knew the Juice Jumper and told me her location, and in the process identified several mutual friends I would meet down the rows of merchants and morning shoppers.

To no real surprise, a line had formed for Della, the juice lady. I shared the timely referral from the mutual friend and began by saying I needed a kale-cure, something to wipe out my lung cancer before it took over my body and my attitude. A juiced-up discussion began with everyone in line sharing stories about her product, my cancer journey, and even my love of goats. Forty years earlier, I'd given my new bride a pregnant Nubian as a wedding present in exchange for a pheasant-directed Remington 870. Our South Dakota homesteading had produced not only goat milk and goat cheese, but it had also introduced me to the contradiction of gentlemen farming and workaholic administrator. "Midnight oil" became a metaphor for milking our very unhappy goats too long after dark after returning late from the university office.

One of the ladies in line owned a goat farm in Virginia, harbored a dislike for Nubians who mounted every vehicle on her property, but loved our reminiscence across "Dairy Goat Guide," delivering baby goats and failed goat cheesecake.

I smiled all the way home from the market. Blueberries and Nubians filling my so-far un-developed electronic brain image. Friendly people and story sharing would always trump intransigent politicians and uncertain medical worries.

As I neared my favorite locally owned bakery where rosemary and goat cheese biscuits were a specialty, followed by blueberry scones, I pulled in knowing they were the first to disappear. Indeed, all their pastries were gone. Empty handed, I left, still smiling. It was a good day for small businesses, new friends, and old friends. A good day for new attitudes. A good day to be fully alive. •

Bill Donohue is a Winston Salem, North Carolina, writer who has chronicled many of his family's medical speed bumps. Recognizing his own aging leaks, rusts, and mold, this story is the first capture of his newest frailty and the beginning of his journey with cancer.

In the End, Timing Is Everything
by Nick Sipe

A bout once a week, I still expect she'll call me.

And I expect she'll call at the worst possible time. When I've finally found childcare and I'm on a date with my wife for the first time in months. Or during the workday when I'm leading an important meeting. When I'm in a movie theatre and the two leads are about to kiss or fight, or both if it's a superhero movie. Or during the middle of preparing dinner when I'm about to plate all the food together at just the right time so that everything stays hot. But she doesn't call anymore. She's gone.

The last time I saw her alive, *truly* alive, she was propped up in her bed, sewing Christmas ornaments. Needles, fabric rolls, scissors and spools were piled up in the empty space where there had once been a leg, now long since amputated. I told her that if she needed more space for crafting, she might need to amputate the remaining leg. She laughed, gave me the finger, and went back to sewing.

Scotch taped over the bed was a laminated picture of a smoldering Jason Momoa, reading, "My ideal weight is Jason Momoa on top of me." The equivalent of a trashy poster in a men's dorm room, it would have been in poor taste even there. It was even more out of place in a nursing home. *She* was out of place in a nursing home.

At 65, she was far younger than the other residents. She asked for more than the other residents, cursed more than the other residents and got into more trouble than the other residents. My aunt, Teresa, or Sis as I'd called her my whole life, loved being the "cool kid" in the nursing home. She roamed the halls in her wheelchair the way an upperclassman roams the halls of their high school. And just like a high school senior, she was often roaming the halls looking for trouble.

Trouble for her meant arguing with the administrator for eating up their WiFi streaming Netflix. (Not allowed.) Or wheeling into the staff kitchen with elaborate excuses to use the oven. (Restricted to staff only.) Or asking me for contraband like a Dremel tool, which she claimed was for crafting, but I suspect was for modifying her furniture. (Power tools are forbidden.) Or for convincing the staff to bring in takeout food during COVID lockdown. (*Strictly* forbidden.)

Somehow in the middle of all this, she always found time to call me, her *favorite nephew*, (her only nephew), to ask what sports my kids were playing, what awards they'd gotten at school, and to ask about me. She always asked about me, even in the middle of nursing home hijinks or new, mysterious ailments.

After 30 years of her mystery ailments, I had learned to block them out mostly. We had trodden those grounds before. Kidney failure. Heart surgery. Diabetes. Cigarettes. Leg amputation. Painkiller addiction. When the final ailment arose, a sore tunneling deep into her ass, (her words not mine), I barely took notice. I only noticed that she started calling less. When the next call came, it wasn't from Sis, it was from Hospice, telling me she'd taken a turn for the worse.

Her last days weren't spent cracking dirty jokes, breaking the rules or sweet talking the nurses, they were spent with her eyes closed, struggling against unseen forces pulling at her. I visited every day, and as I sat with her, holding her hand, and talking, I could not be sure she was hearing me. There was no indication, other than an occasional hand squeeze. I only hoped that when her time came, I would not be in the middle of work, a movie, or dinner. When it mattered, I wanted our timing to finally be right.

Death came calling around 10 a.m. on a Friday morning. I was with her, holding her hand, stroking her hair. She opened her eyes one last time and looked up at the ceiling, awestruck. I asked, "What is it? What are you seeing?" There was no answer and then she was gone.

I sat with her a long time, knowing that I needed to notify the staff that she had passed, but I had no words. I felt so alone, her only family there with her in her final moments. One of the nurses came in to get her water, and seeing her grief, strong and immediate as my own, I hugged her. We cried in each other's arms. Then I did the same with the next one, and the next, and even the administrator. They were her family too, loving her for always breaking the rules.

In the end, when it mattered, we got the timing right. •

Nick Sipe lives in Gastonia, North Carolina, with his alpha-reader wife and two beta-reader kids. He is a member of the Charlotte Writers Club and NC Writers' Network. He enjoys the giddy thrill of sneaking into college libraries to write while his kids are at sports practice. Currently, Nick is querying literary agents for his debut novel, "Midnight Springs," a horror Western best described as "Frankenstein goes out West."

The Jig Is Up

by Arlene Mandell

Arlene Mandell
2023

Morbid curiosity lured me to glance through the repugnant content of the hideous booklet, then shove it into the farthest reaches of my desk drawer. Eventually, I would have to read it, but there was time. I was not yet ready.

"Gone From My Sight, the Dying Experience" by Barbara Karnes was a small, skinny 13-page booklet of guidelines describing bodily changes prior to death, from the final three months to the last day. It was given to me when I signed the paperwork entering my mother into hospice at the nursing home where she lived.

At 95, Mother had been engrossed in activities there with friends she had grown to cherish. That was about to change following a diagnosis of terminal stomach cancer. I conferred in-depth with her much-loved and experienced doctor; we agreed on palliative care and hospice.

I dared not tell Mother. She was terrified of what she called "The Big C," having watched her family suffer slow, torturous deaths from cancer. I contacted no one on the outside; a flurry of phone calls would have sent up a red flag. Even with mild dementia, Mother was shrewd enough to have figured it out.

Sharing my plan with the plethora of staff who would be entering Mother's room and life, I was adamant they were *not* to mention "cancer." If Mother questioned her condition, I said, just say she was being treated for a stomach bug. Only one forgetful staffer, by mistake, blurted out the "cancer" word. However, an episode of dementia had kicked in, and the monstrous six-letter word sailed over her head. In that tense situation, dementia proved, paradoxically, to be a godsend.

Mother and I had never spoken about death until Dad had passed. Transporting his body to the family gravesite in another state had been complicated and an enormous expense. Mother's practical wisdom took me aback: "I will tell you this only once," she said. "When I die, handle it in whatever way is good for *you.*"

With new people parading in and out of her room, Mother, in time, grew suspicious. One afternoon, when we were alone, she burst out, "Is the jig up?" I was flummoxed but kept a poker face—relieved when she quickly followed with, "Wait! Don't tell me!"

Thereafter, I spent every day at Mother's bedside. Groggy, as a continuous diet of morphine took hold, Mother, nevertheless, kept herself tethered to my hands, squeezing them tightly while we listened to her favorite music on my audio player. Every evening, I tenderly pried her hands off mine and kissed her goodnight.

SOONER OR LATER

One night as she lay half-asleep, Mother started tugging at her robe—a peculiar, new behavior. My thoughts flashed back to a phrase in that dreaded, hidden booklet. "Picking at bedclothes" was one of several signs that the body is preparing for death.

It was time. That night, I plucked the guidebook out of my desk and devoured it. I needed to understand what was happening and why, and what more to expect. The words, simple and sympathetic, fell like gentle rain on my frayed emotions.

A day later, surrounded with soft music and with hands entwined in mine, Mother, for the first time, pulled her hands away. Startled, I reached out for her, then snapped back. The booklet explained that the body prepares for its next journey by withdrawing from the outer world and going inward. In that poignant moment, a painful act of love compelled me to best help my mother by letting her go. It was the hardest thing I've ever done.

In the early morning hours, Mother departed this world under the watchful eyes of hospice staff who embraced me when I arrived, assuring me her passing had been serene. A mournful cry rose up throughout the nursing home. The frantic director asked if I could come to the conference room that afternoon. She would have Mother's friends brought there for a Q&A talk. I agreed.

At 2 o'clock, the conference room was jampacked. Questions abounded. I called on Ethel, mother's diminutive and dearest friend, who asked, "I've been wondering, did you two always get along so well together?"

I bellowed a resounding "NO!" Laughter exploded the tension, tears filling the room. I explained that, as an adult, and though reluctant, I had returned to live with Mother. Circumstances decreed we needed to combine our limited financial resources. Over time, our initial guarded civility grew roots into deep understanding and appreciation.

How the body responds to its final journey has an order and a purpose—a comforting thought as I seek order in a chaotic world. Now in my 80s and losing friends I had lunch with only a short while ago, I am acutely aware that my own mortality is in the offing.

And though I'm not ready at the moment, I'm hoping I will be—whenever the jig is up. •

Arlene Mandell is an artist living in Linville, North Carolina, proudly celebrating her 10th year at Carlton Gallery in Banner Elk. (carlton-gallery.com/arlene-mandell). A native New Yorker, relocating to the Blue Ridge Mountains with Captain Dan ignited a passion to write. Her "6-minute Stories" podcasts include: "Eye of the Dolphin," "Artist Borne," "Gobsmacked in the Gulfstream," "Renegade Daughter," "It Started with a Typo," "Shopping for the Homeless," "Thirteen Candles in the Dark," "The Promise of Romance," "At Five & Ninety-Five, Mother Was a Star," and "In the Heart of Trauma."

Banana Bread
by Edith Gettes

Hannah did not answer my knock, but I opened the door anyway. She sprawled on the bedroom floor in her green fleece bathrobe. A towel perched absurdly atop wet hair. Propped up on her elbows, she huddled over the painting she hoped to finish tonight and hang in her new dorm room tomorrow. Burning incense complicated the smell of marijuana, and Aretha Franklin spun gold from a thrift shop phonograph. Surrounded by macerated tubes of oil paint, my middle daughter sang along to "Say a Little Prayer" as she worked. Fireflies glittered against a black sky, rodents rustled in dry leaves outside the window, and moths buzzed harmoniously against its screen.

Knowing she had been nervous about her last day home, I asked how it went. She shrugged. "I got up before noon, showered, dressed, went to the barn, played the piano, finished packing, and...," turning towards me with a smirk, "was delightful at my goodbye dinner with family." I laughed in agreement. An urge to ask whether she had also swigged from the wine under her bed, or the Tussin DM hidden in her closet uncoiled, then morphed into soundbites from the lullaby I wrote for her some 18 years before. "...*Stars are twinkling in the skies, now rest your head and close your eyes...*" She waved me out to "The House That Jack Built."

When I got upstairs, her dad was already in bed. He pulled me close, and I settled into the world's most comforting place. Our breath deepened and slowed until familiar sounds infiltrated from below. Slippers scuffled against the floor; the refrigerator door opened, and leftover containers shifted about; the icemaker groaned, cubes crashed into glass; the microwave hummed and chimed. Moments later, dishes clattered into the sink, and plastic heels click-clacked nervously between bedroom and bathroom, bathroom and bedroom. Hannah was going out.

Almost a year earlier, after she totaled our second car in a late-night foray, we started sleeping with the keys and turning off the internet. Over and over, her compulsion for friends and an altered state outsmarted, or outlasted us. The driveway crackled under her BFF's '91 Ford Ltd Sedan; voices flickered, metal doors slammed, and gravel crunched again. We surrendered to her absence.

I awoke to the resident bluebird irritably pecking his reflection in our bedroom window. A 3:45 a.m. text from Hannah revealed she was home. After a walk, I embarked upon my ritual of making chocolate-chip-banana bread before a trip. Aside from using up ripe bananas, and conjuring a beloved travel snack, the measuring, pouring, melting, mashing, and mixing quelled my anxiety and swaddled me in generations of subconscious memories ... *Mom making haystacks with her mother, me making cookies with mine, and 4-year-old Hannah standing next to me on a stool, singing as sticky little hands squeezed ripe bananas from soft, black peels*—like paint from a tube.

She emerged from her room into sweet, moist banana-bread fog. A rumpled turquoise *Ride aWay Stables* T-shirt hung limply off her shoulders. Fashionably torn jeans pretended to cover her legs and wavy amber hair framed a sleep-deprived face. Dad offered breakfast, but she just wanted to pee and stay in bed until time to go.

Seated across from us at the airport gate, she checked her phone, then slithered her slender body under the armrests and across the cold vinyl seats. I offered my jacket as a blanket or pillow. "No thanks, I'm fine," she said, and turned her back.

A jarringly cheerful flight attendant greeted us at the plane door and suggested we sit together in back. But Hannah, who despised sitting near the toilets, spotted a window seat near the front. "Bye mom," she blurted, stumbling over two seated passengers and flopping into the vacant space by the window. I dug the foil-wrapped loaf from my bag and offered it to her. She was already leaning on the plane's curved shell, eyes closing. "No thanks; see ya."

A torrent of feelings, thoughts, and questions swept over me after we seated ourselves obediently at the rear. *Can this be right? Where is she headed? What should we do?* I closed my eyes and sank deeper into warring currents of fear, hope, doubt, pride, and trust, buoyed by turbulent love. The plane sliced forward.

Our captain's voice boomed overhead just before landing, and

I looked up, aware of a figure gliding towards me. Hannah maneuvered quickly down the aisle. Her dark, impish eyes latched onto mine, while they also scanned mischievously for any flight attendant who might object to her being unbuckled. She reached me, smiled, and presented her hand. "Your jacket and banana bread, please?"

I happily gave them up, then watched her gambol back to her row. My heart, dancing with hope and possibility, hovered close behind. •

Edith Gettes has worked as a professional violinist, teacher, and psychiatrist. Her most important and inspiring employment, however, has been raising four daughters. She has lectured about learning, trauma and motherhood at several international conferences, and her writing has appeared in both musical and medical journals. Edith currently lives, works, plays, and writes in Asheville, North Carolina, where she remains fascinated by our capacity for love and beauty in the face of profound challenges.

Time Will Fool You
by Kenneth Chamlee

With one foot in the eastern hemisphere and one foot in the western, my son and I straddled the Prime Meridian at the Royal Observatory in Greenwich, United Kingdom. It is a fantastic complex, with a maritime museum, art gallery, planetarium, the Cutty Sark sailing ship, and, of course, the galleries dedicated to establishing Greenwich Mean Time and clocks that would keep accurate time at sea.

It was 2004, my son had just graduated from high school, and a trip to England was a gift from his grandmother and me. Graduation being a signature event, a mark of passage on one's timeline to adulthood, it seemed appropriate to visit the very spot where time and longitude are set for the whole world.

Taking trips together was nothing new for Andrew and me, though this was our first one overseas. Since my divorce five years earlier, I had tried to keep some continuity from his childhood on our weekends and summers. We rafted the Nantahala River, camped at the Outer Banks and in the Adirondacks, rode horses in West Virginia, and toured the settlements at Williamsburg and Jamestown.

Time Will Fool You

We used London as our base for the first week of that post-commencement treat, each day negotiating the Tube to a new adventure: experiencing the Blitz simulation at the Imperial War Museum, gawking at the sheer vastness of Westminster Abbey and St. Paul's Cathedral, or catching an open-air performance of *A Midsummer Night's Dream* in Regent's Park.

The significance of keeping time was never lost on me as we planned each day toward museum openings and closings, gauging how long it would take to walk from our tube stop to the zoo or to make curtain for *The Woman in Black*. Our second week was a series of one-and-two-night relocations as we left London and traveled west to Stonehenge and Bath. Then we headed south to Portsmouth and toured the D-Day Museum on a wet and whipping day, hard even to stand, and the beach there was nothing but stones. We passed a day in the historic dockyard seeing the excavated *Mary Rose*, Henry the VIII's warship, and walking the decks of Admiral Nelson's flagship, the impressive *HMS Victory*.

When we returned from England, Andrew sailed into the worlds of college and workplace, and our trips together became helping him move or ferry some won't-fit-in-the-car purchase like a second-hand washer or a sofa found at Habitat. From apartment to apartment, rental house to storage unit or the reverse, my pickup truck and utility trailer were in frequent demand.

Before I knew it, nearly 20 years passed. Andrew established a career in communications technology, and I remarried and retired. I remember standing in front of the atomic clock at the Royal Observatory watching the red digits count steadily onward, the even pace of each second changing to the next. But what struck me about that device of extreme precision were the milliseconds rolling in a indistinguishable red blur. I knew they were the familiar numbers of our decimal system, but the tallying speed unnerved me. Watching just one minute of seconds and micro-seconds run by felt like an hour had passed. Time will fool you.

I texted Andrew the other day and asked him what he remembered from that trip nearly two decades ago. He called right away.

"I remember the conveyor belt moving us past the crown jewels at the Tower of London," he said, "and the passion of those chair-preachers at Speakers' Corner. Oh, and that goth pub decorated in spiders and horror movie stuff."

"Yes! I remember eating delicious tandoori at Lord's Indian restaurant," I said. "And that long, uphill walk pulling suitcases along Monmouth Road to reach our hotel in Bath." We chatted a while and then I asked, "Hey, have we made a trip like that since, I mean, just you and me on a vacation or a getaway?"

"No," he said. "I don't think so."

And there it was. Since 2004 we had not gone on a single adventure together, seeing each other only when he would drop by, at family gatherings, or when transportation was requested. How does that happen, I thought, though I knew the answer was both common and complex.

Time Will Fool You

"We need to change that," I said. "What sounds interesting?"

"Niagara in winter," he said right away. "Always wanted to see it frozen over."

"Sounds good. Let's make a point of it." And though it was easy to say, a maxim trite and true, I added, "We just have to make the time." •

Kenneth Chamlee's work has appeared in five previous Personal Story Publishing Project anthologies. His latest collections are *If Not These Things* (Kelsay Books, 2022) and *The Best Material for the Artist in the World*, a poetic biography of 19th-century American landscape painter Albert Bierstadt (Stephen F. Austin State University Press, 2023). Ken lives in Mills River, North Carolina, and is an active member of the North Carolina Poetry Society and the North Carolina Writers' Network. Learn more at www.kennethchamlee.com.

One More Try
by Jon Kesler

In stark contrast to the minus-30-degree temperature outside, it was hot in the garage. Too hot. The old furnace only had two settings, "off" and "full blast," so following my brother Keith's lead, I peeled off my jacket and flannel shirt and set back to work on his 1962 Jeep Forward Control or "FC" for short. If you know what one of those is, you are a certified Jeepophile. Think a one-quarter scale, old-school Peterbilt cabover with the engine between the seats and you'll get the picture.

Keith was a mastermind under the hood. I was his able-bodied apprentice, grabbing tools at his request, holding the light just so, and being as helpful as I could be. He had a way of teaching me about the art of Jeep maintenance as only a brother could, constantly giving me coaching tips like, "Get the hell out my light," or "I said a box wrench numb nuts," and one of my favorites, "You must have been adopted."

The figurative *we* fiddled with the engine for what seemed like hours, with him doing the work and me pretending to watch intently while daydreaming about whatever an 8-year-old daydreams about when they have absolutely no interest in what they're doing but want badly to impress the one they're doing it with. The evening dragged on. Fiddle a little. Fire it up. Listen. Grunt. Shut it off. Fiddle some more. Repeat.

Without me picking up on any discernable difference between this start and the last, his grunt turned to a smile, and he exclaimed, "Hot damn, I think that did the trick. Let's go road test." I was ready for that. Road tests frequently ended at the little "choke-and-puke" where Keith's blonde "Barbie" worked. He'd get me a treat, so they'd have time to make goo-goo eyes. As for me, I won't say I was motivated by treats, but all my clothes did come from the Monkey Wards Husky Boys aisle.

Opening the garage door, the cold air hit me like a brick. Keith backed out. I hit the lights, pulled the door down, and dove into the cab. He hadn't put the engine cover back on and the heat coming off the manifold warmed me like a campfire. For reasons I can't recall but I'm sure made sense at the time, we left the highway and drove down a back road. Who was I to question? Heck, for all I knew maybe this was a shortcut to a hot fudge sundae.

Several miles in, the little Jeep sputtered, then popped, and finally with a bang and a hiss, all went silent. Instantly, the cold blasted in. Keith looked at me in my t-shirt, jeans, and street shoes, and I looked at him in his. The look on his face did not need translation. It clearly stated, *Oh shit.* More quickly than he had worked in the warm garage, he fiddled with the engine. Turned the key. Nothing happened. Fiddled some more. Turned the key. Nothing. Repeat.

The tingling in my ears, nose, fingers, and toes told me we were in trouble. Keith was having difficulty turning the little adjustment screw on the carb as his fingers began to numb. That sent even more of a chill down my spine. We had left home dressed for a summer day. We didn't tell anyone we were leaving or where we were going. We were several miles down a road that likely wouldn't see another car until morning. And the temperature was still dropping.

Characteristically decisive and quick to action, Keith said, "Here's what we're going to do" and he laid out the plan. The Jensen's had a dumpy little hunting shack about a mile further down the road. We were going to abandon the Jeep and beat feet for the shack, break in, and light the stove. With any luck, we'd find some blankets and hunting clothes. We'd hole up until dad found us or we'd walk out in the morning when it warmed up. The consequences were clear and with a trembling lip, I nodded my understanding.

Keith started to get out as I hesitantly reached for my door handle. He paused, muttered something under his breath, maybe a prayer, but more likely a curse. He pulled his door shut and said, "Wait. Let's give it one more try." Without even taking time to fiddle, he turned the key. In reverse order of how she died, the Jeep gave a hiss, a bang, a pop, and a sputter as it came to life.

We drove home without speaking, the engine noise music to our ears. Keith parked. We both went in the house, hit the cookie jar, and retreated to our respective bedrooms, never saying a word. •

One More Try

Jon Kesler lives in Greensboro, North Carolina, with his wife, Martha, and his Chocolate Lab, Rooster. As an organization development consultant, Jon has made a career of studying people as individuals and how they interact in groups. Writing for his own enjoyment and the entertainment of others, Jon strives to bring his characters to life through the exploration of personality quirks and the underlying dynamics of what makes people tick in the day-to-day realities of life.

Balms

by Jennifer M. Szescula

I am melancholy over the trees. The grey day mixes with grey trees out my back kitchen window. I imagine those trees are covering the mountains I want rolling behind my house. My weather station, the small beige glass table on the back deck, tells me it's started to softly rain. The sky is crying when I cannot.

I move through my morning, puttering. I want to cry. It's a familiar feeling. I felt that way for years in my marriage and for years after my divorce.

Looking out my front bedroom window, I see where trees used to be. A brand-new house stands there now. The new neighbors are lovely people and I have nothing against them. But the trees are gone. Those trees held me through my violent separation, divorce, and years of working 2-3 jobs just to clear off my ex-husband's debts. It came out of nowhere so suddenly, yet the signs were there (just like my failed marriage.) The trees were there when I left one day. And when I returned, it was a desolate patch of red clay and rocks. I never got to say good-bye, never got closure. Not just with the trees.

I walk toward my bathroom window, staring out at my make-believe mountains. There is a large branch in the middle of the yard that fell standing straight up, sticking out of the ground and the leaf piles, a gift from a wildly cold winter storm in early December. I left it there, just like the leaves. I find myself greeting it each time I look out the window and it makes me smile.

Getting dressed, I take off my oil clothes and check my skin. It's been weeks since I oiled, and my skin has plumped and softened under the treatment. I experience ease and anguish in seeing how soft it is but also knowing that it now takes extra work to get it so. I undress completely, taking in my body and bringing my nose to my shoulder. It's the beginning of "the smell."

I'm rounding 41 from 40, and every once in a while I smell it—the fact that I'm closer to death than birth. I smelled the fullness of it on my mother almost 12 years ago now. I was married, living in a house of comfort and isolation with my then husband. Our relationship was troubled. (Actually, all my relationships were.) I hugged her before bed one night, the smell overtaking my brain and hammering me with one thought "She's going to be gone soon." Then I remembered that same smell on my grandmother, how it made me want to run and avoid her apartment as a child.

I take comfort (surprising even myself) that I am beginning to smell like they did (like Mom sometimes still does.) I look at my 40-year-old body in the mirror. It is supposedly 50-60 lbs. overweight according to a medical science that's been disproven for years yet persists somehow. I have no scars that show. My body has not birthed children and likely never will. Still the weight of my breasts hangs low along with the three rolls from my stomach. I carry my scars and my trauma in that weight. And after years of doing battle with my body—losing weight and gaining more back—I just don't care anymore. My body knows what it is doing and what it needs. Everyone, and myself, just need to leave it alone.

I dress in my uniform of jeans and sweater and finish the cleanup of a quiet Saturday morning. I am still melancholy with the previous thoughts in my head, bringing up old memories, forgotten dreams and bright futures. I want to sob still, visualizing the trees I used to see through the windows of the house as I pass through each room.

I have entered the time of re-remembering, of integrating the things I had thought I integrated and processed with thousands of hours and dollars of therapy. I am realizing that the time left for me is short. What am I gonna do with it? Though I bucked the system more than most, I still spent (and spend) most of my days in a quiet unassuming compliant complacency. And even then, I still want to take more naps.

I realize (like all women before me), that this was not the life I dreamt. But I am here, and I am grateful. I will want to run away from it all screaming one day and the next be so grateful I'm in sobbing tears about it. I take comfort in the women before me who have the scars, the dreams, "the smell." In age, in anguish, in shame and in sadness I am not alone. •

Balms

Jennifer M. Szescula, of Lewisville, North Carolina, feels most at home surrounded by trees and mountains. She has written voraciously her whole life, sharing in bursts of enthusiasm (thanks to Winston Salem Writers!) along with decades of silence. Though she desires to write fiction, her natural voice is found writing about the everyday moments and challenges of being human. She is always trying something new-which gives her eternal writing material.

SOONER OR LATER

We Amphibians

by Mark K. Marshall

A sage advisor once referred to me as an amphibian, someone who evolved the ability to live in and appreciate two very different worlds—the deep roots of over 100 years of family history and coming of age in Richwood, West Virginia, a small town enshrouded by the Monongahela National Forest, and the rest of the wide world.

I imagine that for frogs and turtles it's an effortless transition from creek to shore. But for me it's often complicated – melding the past and present, ancient and cutting edge, honor and betrayal, despair and hope, love and shame.

Over time, Richwood declined from a gem nestled along the Cherry River into a hollowed-out remnant of the past as though the forest was trying to reclaim her. It's a fate familiar to small towns in every state: towns devastated by floods; the hospitals, banks, and schools closed; Main Streets lined by darkened, smudged, empty windows; a dwindling population and tax base.

That sage later reminded me that it must take a very strong and devoted person to choose to stay in Richwood. Unlike them, we amphibians come and go. Now a new generation of those who love, honor, and draw strength from that place tend to sprouting shoots of hope and gratitude, two of the things that can help get you through the toughest of times.

Since leaving Richwood, I have traversed those two worlds many times—the glory-whoop I let out when I cross over the Ohio River from Kentucky into West Virginia, and then the lift I feel when freeing myself from the bonds of the past as I begin my return to Tennessee.

When I leave, every foot of the short drive through Richwood seems like a monument to memories from my life. The lumber stacks I walked past every day going to school. The soda fountain in the News Stand where my buddies and I would pump nickels into the jukebox as quickly as possible, furiously scrawling lyrics to songs our band wanted to learn. My Aunt Madge's store on Main Street. The post office where Uncle Jack was postmaster. The intersection of Oakford and Main, where our high school band always tried mightily but unsuccessfully to stay in straight lines while marching around the corner. Calvary Methodist Church, where I was raised. Cemetery Road, where our family plot lies quietly gazing across the valley.

Every time I travel back and forth, I recognize the exact spot where that sense of freedom and renewal of leaving always lifts me. About a quarter mile past the Richwood city limits, I pass into the unincorporated town of Fenwick. Whatever vehicle I'm driving at any given chapter of my life moves me down the two-lane highway hugging the side of the mountain while sweeping above the neighborhood rested along the banks of the river valley. I've passed from creek to shore once again.

Somewhere along the way, those emotional journeys retreat to a tired, empty, anxious guilt of having left everything and everyone behind as I pass by Kentucky towns like Ashland, Morehead, Judy, Stringtown, Booneville, and Cave City. Towns I will likely never visit, me an alien among all those people who would forever remain strangers. I wonder, "Why am I leaving again?" "Where am I really going?" But by the time I pull into my driveway in Nashville, I am at peace with the choices I've made and the place I have long since called home. That is, until I'm inevitably drawn back toward my ancestral home again.

I've matured from the barefoot four-year-old sitting on broken concrete where the sidewalk ended right in front of our house, bawling because my mother had again hidden my shoes so I wouldn't run off after my big brother. It was a gentle but sneaky way to protect me from wandering off too soon. Time has since shaped me into the well-worn man who left long ago, now living among swarms of people from far and wide, many of them amphibians, too. They likely also hunger for the left-behind world, then long for their present-day world once they've made their return.

I was the kid who loved my home and my people but was always ready to run off into the world beyond the end of the sidewalk. Meantime, many others I grew up with rested comfortably in the dreams of staying in a place they love. Despite these journeys through time, I still see the world through the eyes of a small-town kid always expecting to see a familiar friendly face around every corner as I move from creek to shore. •

Mark Marshall moved to Nashville in 1977 from his home state of West Virginia. He has worked mostly as a career coach where he has gotten to hear and share stories with thousands of people from every conceivable walk of life. He now works in private practice and as a career coach at UpRise Nashville. He's also a member of The River Writers. Much of his writing draws upon how growing up in Richwood, West Virginia, a small lumber and mining town deep in the West Virginia mountains, has shaped his life.

To Those Who Wait

by Jane Satchell McAllister

Waiting comprises an inevitable element of travel, whether for planes or trains, museums, events, restaurants, the perfect photo opportunity, or simply breaks in the weather. Having a fairly low patience quotient, I tend to occupy my time with people watching or reading up on what we are about to experience, thus ensuring that the waiting generates something of value or interest. Often, the unexpected things we encounter deliver the greatest delight.

Our visit to the city of Catania on the island of Sicily delivered far more than expected. Not generally a tourist destination, Catania offers easy access to day trips to Mount Etna and the resort town of Taormina as well as the international airport from which we would begin our return home.

The San Nicolo l'Arena church and its famous meridian line served as the primary target of our day in Catania. On the way, we stopped at the Church of Saint Francis of Assisi all'Immaculata. Men in tuxedos and women in bridesmaid dresses of soft coral with zigzag hemlines wandered across the front terrace and on the lava stone staircase. Several photographers stood waiting. Seeing weddings unfold on our travels

To Those Who Wait

serves as a wonderful reminder that the sites we experience as visitors are homebase to locals. As testimony, I consistently marvel at the likely practiced ability of brides to navigate safely tall stone staircases while wearing long gowns and high heels.

I dared to enter the church, though ready to leave as soon as the wedding began. A groomsman approached and asked, in lovely English, if I had visited the church previously. Receiving my reply to the negative, he offered to walk me around the interior and to share its history. I assured him that I did not wish to intrude on the wedding. With a smile, he explained the local custom of the bride arriving late for her own wedding—keeping the groom waiting for some undefined period.

Of particular interest to me inside the rich Baroque church were the dozen statues lining the side aisles, each one 20 feet high and highly stylized. My groomsman guide explained that local guilds in the 1700's sponsored the creation and placement of the statues, hoping for favor perhaps both divine and commercial. I thanked him for sharing his insights and he left me to meander on my own. I returned outside in time to see the bridal limousine coming down the street toward the church some 20 minutes past the scheduled hour.

The bride linked arms with her proud papa, her long white veil fanned out across the red carpet lining that tall stone staircase, as both professional and amateur photographers clicked away. Together, the wedding party entered the big double doors of the church, leading to a moment that would change that bride's life, her groom awaiting her arrival at the altar. I found myself sending out a wish that their years together would be filled with joy, while also reflecting that I rather liked the idea of making the groom wait on his bride. Patience and anticipation build character and seed joy. Seems to me that wedding-day practice sets a good precedent for a durable marriage.

We continued along our way to San Nicolo l'Arena, arriving a few minutes before noon. We wandered the vast interior and drew closer to what we had come to see—the beautifully crafted meridian line that spanned the front transept. Red stone zodiac signs and dates for each day of the year straddled the long center line. A six-inch circle of light appeared on the floor some 15 inches away from the meridian line. Then I realized that circle was the midday sun streaming through the small aperture in the dome. The circle was making its way toward the meridian line. We stood transfixed for an hour as the circle slowly approached the line where it would cross exactly at today's date, a calendar entry that had been laid out and incised 180 years before.

At the instant the light touched the line, my heart skipped, and my grin reached ear-to-ear as we witnessed this astronomical marvel. We had not purposely timed our visit to see this phenomenon but happened to arrive in the right place at the right time.

The front door guard soon wandered back to begin shooing visitors out of the church at the normal closing time of 1:00 p.m., but seeing how excited I was, he turned around and walked back to the front doors, allowing us to stay for the whole cycle. When we did leave, I thanked him profusely for his kindness.

This episode ranks as one of my most favorite travel experiences, one that we might well have missed had we not serendipitously happened upon that wedding-in-waiting. Patience and anticipation had indeed brought us joy. •

Jane Satchell McAllister's writings draw inspiration from the wide variety of people and places she encounters, from her home base in Davie County, North Carolina, to rich adventures across our country and abroad. She has co-authored two Images of America books through Arcadia Publishing and served for nine years as director of the county public library. Her current writing project is compiling stories based on decades of travel, both fiction and nonfiction, almost as much fun as the trips themselves.

Angels in Disguise

by Janice Luckey

"I absolutely won't have strangers in my house," my mother-in-law said years ago when the family approached her about hiring caregivers for what would turn out to be the last year of her life. She was adamant, jaw set, eyes narrowed, "I don't want anyone rifling through my belongings." Why was she being so obstinate? I wondered. What was the big deal?

The big deal we came to understand intimately when faced with hiring caregivers for my husband after a fall from a ladder left him paraplegic. It was a very big deal. Feelings ran deeper than simply not wanting strangers touching our stuff. Allowing caregivers and a host of health care workers into our home was a complex emotional issue involving not only our physical lives, but our mental, spiritual, and financial lives as well. We opened ourselves up to a myriad of tiny daily invasions.

Biblical scripture, however, teaches we should be hospitable to strangers as they may truly be angels in disguise. I took this admonition to heart when two caregivers, Marta and Sal, entered our lives as strangers, but were in fact angels who appeared at just the right time to meet our deepest need.

My plans to be my husband's primary caregiver were short-lived. Three weeks after he came home from the hospital, I fractured my vertebra. Unable to attend to his basic physical needs, we began looking for caregivers. Enter Marta, our first stranger/angel. She was dark haired and dark eyed, but the rest of her facial features were obscured by a COVID face mask. This only added to her mysterious demeanor. She rarely spoke as she went about her tasks, her petite feet padding through the house, helping to knit our convulsed life back together. She so gently folded us into her tranquil care, she conjured up an image of a geisha of old, her scrubs a kimono.

Taking care of all my husband's needs was her priority, but she filled the rest of her hours setting our household in order. She took care of our needs before we knew they were needs. Marta's efficiency gave me much needed time to deal with the other aspects of our fractured life—medical bills, insurance claims, prescriptions, doctor's appointments, transportation—and to breathe. Marta was indispensable, and I know I never would have survived those first horrific months without her. She came to us in the fullness of time—exactly who we needed exactly when we needed her. Then she was gone.

After a long line of less-than-stellar caregivers came and went, we were frustrated and worn out by the lack of consistent help. Months went by with no outside help other than family and friends who were stretched thin. We were on the verge of emotional bankruptcy when Sal, our next stranger/angel burst onto the scene. Whereas Marta was quiet, Sal was boisterous—a bull-in-the-china-shop variety and looking in no way angelic. He was an older gentleman, large in stature with a thick Brooklyn accent. His face was taken over by a Jimmy Durante snozz, and he quite often smelled of salami. We soon learned he had "two left feet" and tripped over everything with his giant orthopedic shoes. He joked that Murphy, of Murphy's Law, sat on his shoulder. He was not wrong. But you could set your clock by the man! At that point in our journey, we needed someone responsible and dependable. Sal had that in spades.

We also learned he was somewhat of a savant when it came to movies. No matter how old or obscure the movie, Sal knew the title and the actors. *Straw Dogs?* Dustin Hoffman. *Exodus?* Paul Newman. It became a nightly challenge to stump Sal. We never did. Sal taught us how to laugh again. He, too, came to us in the fullness of time—exactly who we needed to aid in our healing. Then he too was gone.

We take for granted that time is on our side, that each minute, day, month, and year will slip gently over us like a silk nightgown, but all it takes is a single sound—the trill of a phone or the clatter of a ladder—to disintegrate all sense of chronological time. One moment you are safe and sound and the next you are suspended in time, sitting in a grimy lawn chair, watching paramedics lifting your husband from the ground to a stretcher. The sight makes time lose all meaning, and its gravity floats away.

But that is not the end of the story. The Creator of Time knows we need the geishas and the savants to lighten our load and exactly when we need them. Stranger/angels come in Kairos time—the fullness of time. Just the exact right time. Yes, once strangers, but now true angels indeed. •

Angels in Disguise

Janice Luckey, who lives in Mooresville, North Carolina, remembers when writing became a rhythm of her life. She scribbled a romance novel in a 3-ring binder in junior high school sparking a life-long love of all things writerly—writing, reading, journaling and hoarding office supplies. Janice is fueled by the love and support of her family and most anything chocolate. When not writing, she can be found making memories with her husband and four granddaughters, or roaming the aisles at the library, bookstores, and Staples.

Ostriches
by Lisa Williams Kline

We were in our beach cottage on the North Carolina coast, enjoying shrimp from the local fish market that Jeff had prepared with his special seasoning. As we gazed at the golden sunset marsh, I said, "The water in our back yard is higher than it was last summer."

"Maybe a few inches. Not much." With a small shrug, Jeff dipped a shrimp in remoulade sauce.

"Well, it's crept up at high tide about a foot, especially during a full moon. Sooner or later, this little strip of land is going to be underwater." The minute I said it, I regretted it.

"We're having a perfectly nice dinner. It's decades away," he said, impatiently.

"Not that far away. 2050 maybe. During our girls' lifetimes." I refolded my napkin, sorry that I had brought it up.

"There's nothing we can do about it, so what's the point of worrying?"

"It just seems…inevitable. I don't know…should we sell it?"

"Are you kidding me? We love this place!"

"I don't want to sell it, either; I love it as much as you do."

"Let's change the subject. I don't want to think about it, much less talk about it."

I felt bad to ruin our dinner, even with a subject we needed to discuss. My husband had always wanted a beach house, but we could never afford one. After he retired, it became possible. We've owned a little gray cottage on Caswell Beach for several years now and could not love it more. Our daughter Caitlin, when asked once about her idea of Heaven, answered, "The front porch of our family beach house."

The house was built in 1964, with tiny bedrooms and bathrooms, old-fashioned paneling, and what we've come to call a "one-butt kitchen."

The front faces the beach, just across the street. The back faces the marsh. Our marsh view is spectacular, and we never tire of watching the herons, egrets, hawks, and pelicans. I keep trying to capture the view with both photos and watercolors and cannot come close to its breathtaking beauty.

We are not the only ones experiencing the creeping water. One back yard a few doors down turns into a pond during high tide. For the past two years, that neighbor has had truckload after truckload of dirt dumped back there and it just washes away. Others build seawalls and they crumble. After storms now, the road leading to our house is often flooded for two days.

This year our hazard insurance doubled. We had to pay because it's the only company that offers it for properties like ours. Eventually, regular people like us won't be able to afford beach houses. Only those who are wealthy enough to afford the insurance.

As a free-lance writer, I once wrote a nonfiction book on floods, and in my research learned that there are many areas that have flooded multiple times where our government will no longer allow people to rebuild. I remember learning that and thinking, "Well, that makes sense. It's not practical to keep rebuilding in a flood zone."

But now I am a person who owns a beloved cottage in just such a place. A place that, if sea level rise continues, may be underwater.

Since we've owned our cottage, dredging has taken place almost constantly in the strait between our beach and Bald Head Island. Sand has been dumped to fight the beaches washing away. In my research for the book on floods, I learned that if the complex system of dikes, ditches, and canals in Holland were somehow breached, half of the country would be gone. And I recently read that people are having to evacuate islands in Indonesia.

Jeff and I try to do our part to limit our carbon footprint. We have sworn our next car will be electric, or at least hybrid. We seldom fly. I have stopped eating red meat. I use cold water to wash our clothes, and we watch lights and thermostats. We recycle. But unless millions of people do these things, and more, sea levels will keep rising.

Ostriches

83

It gave us tremendous "nachas," as Jeff says in Yiddish,
to think our children might be able to enjoy this sweet place
after we're gone. Of course, this cottage is a second home—
not our only home. And as Jeff says, it's many years away, and
human behavior could change that future.

Now, when we eat dinner at the beach, we don't talk about it.
We watch the water sparkling near the edge of our carport.
We watch the stately egrets wade and hunt, practically
in our backyard.

"Your shrimp is especially delicious tonight," I tell Jeff.

"Thanks," he says. •

Copyright 2023, Lisa Williams Kline

Lisa Williams Kline is the author of two novels for adults,
Between the Sky and the Sea, and *Ladies' Day*, as well as an essay
collection entitled *The Ruby Mirror* and a short story collection
entitled *Take Me*. Her stories and essays have appeared in *Literary
Mama*, *Skirt*, *Sasee*, *Carolina Woman*, *moonShine review*, *The Press 53
Awards Anthology*, *Sand Hills Literary Magazine*, and *Idol Talk*, among
others. She is also the author of ten novels and a novella for young
readers. She lives in Davidson with her veterinarian husband, a cat
who can open doors, and a sweet chihuahua who has played Bruiser
Woods in *Legally Blonde: The Musical*.

The Longest Day
by David Inserra

My wife's body language and the wide-eyed horror on her face confirmed that this was as bad as it felt. All Ellen could do was clutch her crochet bag and watch me being tortured.

A sizable horse tranquilizer needle was filled with numbing medicine and shot into the four X's, marked with a sharpie, on my head. The pain was excruciating. The liquid bubbled around my skull. My skin surged and twisted. I wanted to scream. I wanted to cry out, but I remained quiet. This procedure was by choice.

Two-inch mounds of medicine rose from each injection site. When the doctor came back two hours later, he said "You have a big head. This frame may not fit." To flatten the mounds, he took his spatula-sized thumbs and rammed at the horns, causing crackling, sputtering sounds to echo in my ears. When it was over, I prayed for relaxation, but it was not to be found. He slipped the metal frame over my head, grabbed it tight and screwed four pins into my skull.

I had suffered from double vision for some time. Imagine going to the store and seeing shelves with a hundred yellow tags advertising weekly sales. When I looked at the shelves, I saw two hundred tags. As time passed, the strain on my brain increased and my vision got worse. Headaches. Throbbing and tingling down the side of my face. Discouraging and depressing. No longer able to stand the discomfort, I had an MRI, the results of which changed my life. They found a tumor in my head. This tiny white spot invaded a sensitive area called Meckel's Cave. It exerted pressure on the Cavernous Sinus, a space behind each eye housing six nerves and blood vessels that control the eyes and face. This is what caused the double vision.

The specialists gave me three options. Live with it. Have something called Gamma Knife Radiation, which could take up to two years to see any results. Or a third option of traditional surgery, only recommended if this were a life-or-death situation. In each case, they offered no guarantees that my sight would ever bounce back.

I chose radiation.

Two hours after they attached the frame, I got wheelchaired upstairs for an MRI. A mousy woman wearing a similar frame waited in the elevator. Tiny in her wheelchair, her head drooped, sadness poured from her body, and her eyes stared blankly beyond the elevator walls. I smiled. "This would be a cool gimmick," I said. "Let's form a band."

She studied me for a few beats. Then a grin crept across her lips. "Thank you," she whispered.

This MRI focused on the invader in my head. Once they had a precise 3-D image with tighter slices, they could plan their attack. They screwed my metal frame onto the table and shortly thereafter, the machine started clicking away, grinding, rolling.

Back at the room, Ellen helped me pass the time by teaching me how to crochet. Even with the weight of the frame pulling on my neck, I found myself able to create a one-inch square. I felt proud. It took my mind off this longest day. When my stomach growled—not having eaten since the previous night— I stretched out on the bed and closed my eyes.

Ellen came to my side. She held my hand and we waited.

We arrived at the hospital at 5:30 a.m. I had been wearing the frame since 7:00 a.m.

At 4:00p.m. another wheelchair arrived. They took me to an enormous sterile room. Ten people in white ushered me to the Gamma table. They screwed my head frame onto the device and told me I could cough, move, whatever, it did not matter. My head was so tightly wound, it would not affect the procedure. They offered a choice of music to listen to, so I chose The Beatles. Then the machine inserted my body into a tight white tube, and I waited.

I closed my eyes. I listened. I breathed. I tried to stay calm.

Other than a few clicks and movements, the machine remained quiet. If not for the music, I am sure anxiety and claustrophobia would have filled my chest.

Forty-five minutes later it ended. They released me from the machine and unscrewed the frame from my head. I heard the pins unwinding and I felt my skin pulling and twisting as my freedom closed in.

Ellen hugged me when I returned to the room. They offered a light snack while waiting to see if I would have any reactions from the procedure. At 6:00 p.m. they released us, and I began the wait to see if my vision would ever return.

On the way home we stopped for ice cream.

I had never tasted anything so astonishing. •

Copyright 2023, David Inserra

David Inserra lives on Hilton Head Island, South Carolina with his wife Ellen Titus and their dog, Mindy. David's most recent work appears in the PSPP release, *Lost & Found*. He is a member of the Island Writers Network and works at the local Unitarian Church. David's first novel, a speculative thriller titled "In Your Own Backyard," is currently being queried to agents. He is also a musician who has written over 400 songs, most being about his wife. Visit davidinserra.weebly.com.

Forest Bathing on Horseback
by Janet K. Baxter

A short while ago, my bi-annual bone scan revealed that I am at high fracture risk. My physician strongly recommended that I quit riding my horses to reduce the chance of falling and breaking a hip.

"No," I said impulsively.

She persisted, providing a stream of data to support her recommendation, and implied she'd ask repeatedly that I stop riding.

"Then I'll lie," I said with equal persistence.

As I pondered this gut reaction to my physician's stark recommendation, I found that what I cherish most is to experience nature in its rawness and wonder. I have had experiences that have nurtured my soul. "Forest bathing" on horseback is my mantra as I carefully prepare for each ride.

One year, I found twin fawns nestled between two fallen trees, their mother bounding away in fright. Throughout that year, I often passed the fawns still hidden by the tree trunks. The next spring, they were gone.

Forest Bathing on Horseback

89

Another year, enjoying a cool ride in the early fall, I observed a lone adolescent squirrel swinging on a thin, spindly tree branch, jumping down to the ground, and then scampering up the tree to jump out on the same branch to again bounce wildly up and down. He did this multiple times as I rounded nature's playground in the curve of the trail.

Once, a fledgling bird fell, grazed my right shoulder, and landed softly in the moss and leaves at the foot of an aging oak tree. I turned and sent a silent prayer that his mother was nearby to feed him until he was able to fully fledge.

In early spring, near the creek beds, I hear frogs croaking as they wake from winter's hibernation. Just weeks before, I experienced stillness and quiet as I passed the same spots. Spring also brings out the snakes and I've seen a tangle of black snakes cavorting in the spring warmth and copper heads and rattle snakes sunning on the open, warm spots on the trail. Once, a rather defensive black snake crossed the trail and then curved back in a hostile posture. I gave that one an extra wide berth as I passed by.

Another time, my mare stopped dead in the trail and absolutely refused to go forward. She could sense something, and she was not budging. After quite some time and much coaxing, she decided it was safe enough to continue. More recently a bold coyote stepped across my path, traversed a fallen log, and then continued traveling through the woods like he owned it.

Two experiences always make me smile. Both involve novice hikers enjoying the shared hiking-riding trail. One ride, I found two nice young men in their early-20's who came out of the woods using the fire lane, not the trail itself. We had a nice conversation and then I asked my usual question, "Do you know where you are?"

"Yes!" they enthusiastically answered in unison.

"OK, which way do you go to get back to your car?" And they both pointed in the exact opposite direction of where their car was parked.

On another ride, I passed teens on an orienteering expedition, which means that after a bit of training they had been given a topographical map and were required to find various locations out in the woods. I rode over a mile farther and then heard, off to my left, a whistle blaring the emergency signal of three short, three long, three short blasts. I climbed the hill and from the top of the ridge I called and guided a quite scared 16-year-old to my location. How he got from the orienteering area, across the creek, and up the slope is beyond me, but there he stood pale and shaking. I led him back to the trail and instructed him how to reach his group. I let him return without me to keep his dignity intact.

Two visceral experiences have stayed with me over the years. On one ride, out of the corner of my eye, I saw a large, dark shape swoop down into a clearing. As I turned, I saw an owl fly off above the trees with an impressively large, writhing, rattle snake in its talons. But the most gut-wrenching sight— nature at its most raw—was a fox running a tottering fawn across the trail as the doe was behind stomping and blowing, desperately trying to scare away the fox.

People ask, "You ride alone?" with *you should never ride alone* implied in their tone.

"Yes," I still say.

And, in the back of my mind, I hear my soft inner-voice whisper, *While I still can.* •

Janet K. Baxter lives in Kings Mountain, North Carolina and is a member of the Charlotte Writer's Club and Scribblers, a memoir critique group. Her stories, "Horse Whispering for the Average Woman," "Southern Blues," "A Frank Lesson," "Cappie, The Boomerang Horse," "An Angel's Smile," "Morgan: Our Escape Artist," and "One Soul Alone" appeared in previous anthologies published by the Personal Story Publishing Project. Retired, Janet enjoys thread painting, writing, trail riding, and all the joys from her "mini-estate": www.mountaingaitacres.com.

Crossing Bridges

by Lisa Watts

It is early May in the Florida Keys, but the afternoon has grown as hot and muggy as an August day in North Carolina. A few road signs confirm what the guy told us at the Cuban sandwich shop a ways back: Seven Mile Bridge looms ahead. My gut starts to clench. Soon we see the long ribbon of two-lane highway, arched in its middle for passing ships, that connects two lumps of land in the Atlantic Ocean. Dee and I are heading north, bicycling on the bridge's shoulder. Cars and trucks thunder past, just a few feet to our left. A few feet to our right, a concrete wall not quite as tall as our bike seats is all that stands between us and the ocean. We pedal straight into a stiff, 20 miles-per-hour headwind that slows us to a crawl. I am dehydrated from our 45 miles of biking already today. My arms ache from gripping my handlebars too tightly. I'm afraid to change my hand position for fear of swerving into traffic. Have I mentioned that biking over high bridges terrifies me?

This is not at all how things are supposed to be going. It's the first day of my two-month bike ride up the East Coast with Dee, a friend of three decades. The trip is my big hurrah on the brink of turning 60. For eight weeks I am escaping all the trappings of adult life—job, marriage, parenting, home ownership—to realize a dream I've been fashioning for decades. I want to prove to myself that I am capable of this feat of endurance, biking 3,000 miles from Key West to Canada. But I didn't expect to be tested on Day One. We are wilting in the heat, I got a flat tire in the first few hours of riding, and now the headwinds and this damn bridge.

I define average in so many ways: middle class, late middle age, middle management. Average height, average weight, moderately athletic. All of this pleases the part of me that seeks and values balance. But it also means living a life of mediocrity. The closer I got to 60, the more restless I felt. I had an itch to do something just a bit extraordinary, one thing that was above average. I didn't have to circle the globe singlehandedly; a trip up the East Coast would do.

I could not consider such a trip while I was busy raising kids, moving homes, and meeting work deadlines. Even as an empty nester, the idea of leaving my husband and our dogs to go ride my bike for two months has seemed a bit selfish. But the older I get, the more selfishness morphs into self-care. If there's ever a time to figure out who I am, it's now.

Looking back, five years since my East Coast trip, I see how much those two months on my bike taught me. Some things should have been obvious, like the first day's lesson about how adventures don't go exactly to plan, no matter how many months I spent studying our route and collecting gear.

Other lessons run deeper. I am my best self when I travel, or so I always thought. Even better on a bicycle, where I can become a kid again, playing outdoors all day with no worries except following the route and keeping myself fueled. But living this way for eight weeks, with great expectations riding on the trip, made me face aspects of myself that aren't so appealing: my irritability (especially when hungry) and my fears, from crossing bridges to self-doubt.

By the time we reached the halfway point of Washington, D.C., I knew I could bike 60 miles or so for days on end. It took longer—somewhere between New York City and Maine—for the wisdom of mindfulness to take hold. To survive bridges— none of them as terrifying as Florida's Seven Mile Bridge— I got good at putting my head down and taking it pedal stroke by pedal stroke. More importantly, I learned to navigate the intensity of so many days and nights living within three feet of my old friend—more togetherness than I've experienced even in married life. I forced myself to speak up when I was frustrated, breaking old habits of going quiet or getting passive aggressive. I'm proud of how far my friend and I have traveled over the years, in miles and in life lessons.

At some point, pedaling through New England, I realized I could finally feel with all my senses how it truly is the journey that matters, not the destination. And I understood that I could live this way, more confident in my capabilities and open to possibilities, on and off my bike—as the curtain lifts on life's third act. •

Lisa Watts is a nonprofit communications manager living in Greensboro, North Carolina. She conceived and edited *Good Roots: Writers Reflect on Growing Up in Ohio* (Ohio University Press, 2006), an anthology of essays and poems by 20 prominent writers. She is working on her own essay collection about her two-month bike trip up the East Coast.

For the Ache of Art
by Nell Whitehead

*D*amn, *my feet hurt.* Well, maybe only a little at this point. More like they're numb. It could be my toes are now fused together, as if in the first stages of foot-binding. *Why, oh, why do they have that rule about closed-toe shoes?* Respectable, fashion-forward women in the South paint their toes and show them in unbound comfort—a practice not tolerated here, it seems. Maybe it's a rule aimed at elderly volunteers at the art museum. Perhaps the director and curators are afraid to let the uncovered tootsies of older woman—those gnarled, wizened tree branches adorned with magnetic magenta, or panther pink—be on view next to Ansel Adams or Andrea del Sarto. Ageism, maybe? Or just my biased take as a retired person seeking meaningful activity.

That's me, all right, a recent senior recruit. Brand spanking old but new, in fact. And it's my very first day doing tours at the North Carolina Museum of Art. Got my security clearance for access to the underground tunnel and badge to prove it. Got my code to clock into the computer downstairs, a dark floor a level below the light filled galleries. It's a cavernous space of huge caches of locked-up stored art and pipes and machinery I don't understand. After ascending in the elevator, I'm clicking across the polished floors of the hall behind the restaurant and gift shop and through the main lobby. I arrive for duty at the information desk across from the main entry to the East Building of the North Carolina Museum of Art. That's where I'm standing at this moment.

It is such an honor, such a privilege, to volunteer in this place of treasures! Only it's paid for by the pain of wearing these shoes. The only closed-toed ones that match my outfit. But it's my first day on the job and I'm bound to fit in as best I can amid splendor.

But these shoes, my shoes, made by artisans in Israel, lovely black leather, squared off, tapered closed-toe, kitten-heel, have a comfort limit of only thirty minutes. And it has expired.

It expired during my debut, that fiasco tour I completed only a few minutes ago. But my breathing is almost back to normal, and my memory of the event is upholstered in the cotton wool of shock which helps me forget my shame. I am supposed to be a "Meet-Your-Museum Ambassador," a fancy title I cannot live up to. *Heavy is the head that wears the crown.*

My first tour was an unambiguous ambassador disaster. First of all, about 25 visitors showed up. I was gobsmacked. I was hoping for five at the most. Secondly, they appeared knowledgeable. With me hoping for the ignorant to impress. And third, my confidence in all the notes I made, three pages, studied and memorized in large print on blue graph paper, evaporated. I was dry mouthed in terror. I had not slept the night before. I was certainly jumping into my circle of fear. That's supposed to be good for me. But what about them? Our unfortunate visitors. *Poor them.*

That ordeal, my very first tour, passed in a blur. But still I saw them, our visitors, who I was supposed to be guiding. I saw them yawn, look at each other, their feet, their watches. Although time was slowed for them it was rapidly pressing on me, and I not able to disgorge my voluminous planned information into the paucity of the half-hour time slot. I spewed forth a mash of architecture, history, dates, square footage, pours of concrete, glass, photovoltaic cells, computer operated skylights. I worried about farting, swallowing the wrong way, and maybe peeing just a little in my pants.

Some of the guided, seeing that it was hopeless, wandered away. Eventually almost half peeled off unceremoniously. I plowed on, panting, looking at my watch, trying to cram 167,000 square feet into 30 minutes. If it hadn't been a chilly 58 degrees in there, to protect the art, I would have busted a flop sweat. I dragged them, only mildly protesting, through 5,000 years of art, first striding, then mincing, and at last limping, back to the information desk where I did not have the will to tell them of the reasonable bargain for membership. Only 16 had survived. But the uplifting fact is that I was one of the sixteen. Yay!

And only 28 minutes and a latte before I have to do it all over again. And yeah, did I mention, *my feet hurt?* •

For the Ache of Art
99

Nell Whitehead lives in Wake Forest, North Carolina. She has been writing or teaching writing since childhood. Her family was her first audience when at age 12 she wrote a *Fractured Fairy Tale Christmas*, performed by nieces and nephews, and received with wild acclaim. As a Language Arts teacher, she was part of the *Capital Area Writing Project*. In more recent times, a writing group in Carrboro created by Nancy Peacock has been the inspiration for short stories, memoirs, and two novels.

If You Build It

by Alexandra Goodwin

I suppose they were bound to show up one day to partake from the sanctuary we had intentionally created. Granted, it took 25 years, 7 months, and 13 days, but the stage was set, and their arrival into our backyard made history.

I was working in my home office that afternoon when I heard a clear string of high-pitched whistles I did not recognize. Over the years, bird calls have become familiar to me, and I've learned to identify the multifaceted song of the mockingbird, her trills for nesting, his clucks to mate; the short crystalline whistle of the cardinal; the sobbing coos of the mourning dove; the aggressive shriek of blue jays; even the dainty tweet of the hummingbird.

Puzzled, I walked over to the window. Dozens of brownish grayish birds with rusty red underbelly and yellow beak hopped cheerfully all over the ground, pecking here and there, savoring a feast of worms and insects we never even knew lived in our garden. Excited and impressed by the numbers and camaraderie of the flock, I ran to the bookshelf and opened the *National Geographic Backyard Guide to the Birds of North America*. I leafed through the glossy pages until I landed on the

page with the exact image of the birds in our yard.
The American Robin had finally made an entrance into our
lives! So, what had taken them so long? Why now, after so
many years? Would this mark the beginning of their annual
visit or was this a once in a lifetime gift? The book specified
robins will stop in Florida during the month of February. So
how long would they stay? I took my binoculars and feasted
on the details of their plumage, the wiggling worms struggling
to free themselves from the birds' beaks.

I remembered one winter Sunday when we went to the local
nursery about five years ago looking for plants that attracted
hummingbirds. The owner of the family business—a long-
haired, white bearded poet stuck between the '60s rock-and-
roll and the need to make a living—signaled us to follow him.
We walked among rows of jatrophas, poincianas, and
bougainvillea. A whimsical cottage the color of clouds stood
amid tropical lush bushes. Pastel painted butterflies surrounded
the single four-pane window. The door creaked as we tiptoed
inside in awe. An antique secretary desk with an old *Royal
Electric* typewriter and a stack of letter paper sat in a corner
by the window and for lack of a copy machine there was
carbon paper as well. His poems papered the walls of the doll
house from floor to ceiling, some typed, some handwritten; all
of them tributes to nature, hymns of gratitude to life.

We walked through the cinnamon-scented tiny house and
exited through another door that led to the back of the
nursery, off limits to customers. This was the family's personal
space, a private paradise of ponds, water fountains, turtles,

parrots, and goldfish. It was like stepping into an enchanted rainforest, fragrant with the wet scent of the tropics, cooled off by the misty droplets generated by the water fountains. The Poet gardener pointed to a plant with red tubular flowers, simple and unassuming. Not impressed and rather annoyed (I wanted a burst of colors in front of my kitchen window), we started to walk away, when we heard a dainty squeal. We turned in its direction and held our breath as the iridescent feathers of a hummingbird shimmered in the afternoon sunlight, its beak extracting nectar from the unpretentious red trumpet vine. Captivated, we took two bushes home.

Although it was a while before the hummingbirds found their way to our backyard, eventually they did, and we have been rejoicing in their presence ever since.

A few years ago, when our children flew the nest, we felt the need to replace the warmth and joy that once lived within the walls of our home. We figured that by creating a habitat for birds, we would bring song and color back to our lives. I had read that bluebirds like to nest in wood bird houses called "condos" and in Midwest America it is common to see them posted along fences and poles. Just like the line from the movie *Field of Dreams* asserts, "if you build it, they will come," bluebirds somehow find these nesting structures and make them their own. Last year we hung a bluebird condo from a hook on the fence facing north, between the firebush and the Argentine almond tree, in the hopes that one day bluebirds will discover it and drop anchor there. We now know it's just a matter of time, but we hope it won't take another 25 years! •

Alexandra Goodwin was born in Argentina, and she divides her time at home in Florida between her imaginary tree house in her mango tree and her pool, unless there is a hurricane. Her essays and poems can be found in *Ariel Chart*, *The Centifictionist*, *Loch Raven Review*, *Stick Figure Poetry Quarterly*, *The Miami Herald*, *Twists and Turns*, and *Lost and Found*. This is her third story in the Personal Story Publishing Project. Visit www.alexandragoodwin.com for more information about her and her work.

Parent, Child, Lost

by Linda James

Although role reversal is often gradual as parents become less capable, for me, it occurred suddenly with an unexpected phone call. "Dad's talking gibberish," my mother cried. "I think he had a stroke."

A dropped laundry basket, hugs from my sons, a plane ride north, the drive up the hill to my parents' home on the lake. Mom's voice quivered. "Did I do the right thing?"

"Yes." Shaken, I guided her to her room. "Go pack. Dad's being airlifted to a larger hospital outside Philly."

Emergency surgery relieved pressure from a brain hemorrhage. The doctors pronounced Dad well enough for release once his coherence returned after days in the Intensive Care Unit. They prescribed rest and follow-up despite their inability to identify a cause.

Except for a lone, insistent physician no one wanted to hear. "There's an underlying issue. Take your father to an oncologist."

Weeks later, I sat between my trembling parents facing a somber local specialist. "Ed, your results are back. Your brain bleed is the presenting symptom of blood cancer."

Parent, Child, Lost

Dad froze. Mom began to hyperventilate. The doctor handed me the baton disguised as a pamphlet. *Mantle cell lymphoma: aggressive…rare…incurable…poor prognosis…low five-year survival rate.*

Sweat soaked my shirt as they all looked to me. The shift when parent becomes child, child becomes parent, was complete. I was unwittingly in charge. The doctor urged my parents to stay with me. "We're not equipped to treat this disease locally," he said. "It'll be difficult for your parents to commute the hundred miles to Philadelphia for treatment. UNC Lineberger is an excellent alternative."

So began the difficult years of managing Dad's illness while juggling school, baseball and swimming for my teenage sons. I faced exhausting trips to Pennsylvania, delays getting Dad into the UNC system, all while fighting Mom's denial. A physician friend cut through red tape to schedule my father with a neurologist.

After only three weeks in our house, Mom announced, "We're going home."
I was blindsided. "Dad starts treatment in ten days. You've waited all this time to see the oncologist."
"We leave tomorrow." Dad nodded in agreement.
Contrary to logic, they departed. One month later, she called again. "Your father isn't well. I guess we'll have to return to you." *So much precious time wasted.*

We sold their house and moved them south. Radiation to the brain killed localized malignant cells while altering Dad's personality. The brilliant intellect who once designed equipment to test airplane electronics could no longer decipher a highway interchange. The man I relied on my whole life—

from tying shoes to getting a mortgage—was reduced to an innocent child.

My relationship with my mother grew as toxic as Dad's chemotherapy, our shared fear poisoning mutual tolerance and understanding at the cellular level.

"Why didn't you call me?" she snapped after I tucked Dad into bed.
"We were moving from one appointment to the next," I said, biting my tongue.
"I worried non-stop."
"Then try coming with us for once."
"This apartment's too small."
"Mom, I've been at the hospital for ten hours. This is what you want to discuss?"
"When he's better, we'll need a nicer place," she snipped.

For my mother, I became the face of the disease, the ugly, bossy thing that upended her world. For my father, I became a lifeline.

We pushed the limits of his body and medical science, trying experimental therapy. The call I expected, yet prayed would never happen, came in the dead of night. Blood-soaked Emergency Room doctors entered the near-empty waiting room. "His spleen burst. Does he want extraordinary measures?"
"No life-support machines," Mom said. "He has a living will."
I expected her to disregard the unnotarized document, but she surprised me. "He doesn't want that."

Parent, Child, Lost

Dad died December 22, his own father's birthday. My tears splattered the yellowed note my grandfather wrote when Dad turned eighteen. I found it neatly folded inside Dad's wallet.

Timing can be cruel, disease crueler. Together, they can be malicious. After New Year's, sixteen days after Dad succumbed, my phone rang. "On re-evaluation of Ed's blood work, we see small signs of improvement," his Physician's Assistant said. "The new drug is worth another try." "My dad passed away." *In your hospital's ER. Why don't you know?*

I still lament how the skill, patience, and stamina required to meet my parents' wants eluded me as I struggled to meet their basic needs. "I'm sorry I've become your medical taskmaster," I told Dad in the Community Rose Garden.
He grasped my hand, flashing his goofy smile. "You're just trying to save my life."

We had an 18-month remission where life was good albeit different. When it ended, my frightened father whispered, "I know it's been a lot, but your mother and I really need you."

Roles that blurred and reversed now merged.
"I need you too, Dad. Always have."
Parent…Child…Lost. •

SOONER OR LATER

Time in a Circle
by Carroll Taylor

One summer morning my grandmother waited by her mailbox, fully dressed but barefoot, her pocketbook on her arm, ready to go. Somewhere. Nowhere. My Aunt JoAnn found her and led her back home. My grandmother said an intruder had entered her house and turned on a stove burner. She could not remember how to turn it off. Later she told us she'd seen a chipmunk in the houseplants in her kitchen. We looked everywhere, but there was no chipmunk. My grandmother's slow descent into dementia was beginning.

My mother and JoAnn cared for her during the next few years, first in her home and then in a home-care facility. They watched her become someone they no longer knew. The two sisters forged a special bond, deflecting my grandmother's constant insults while becoming her "mothers" instead of her daughters. Toward the end of her life, she lived in a rural nursing home.

As she lay dying, my grandmother called to my mother as if she were still her young daughter playing outside. In her final days, she called to her constantly, even though my mother was by her bedside. In the hours before her death, she circled back in time and called to her four deceased sisters. She did not call the name of her living sister.

Twelve years later my mother's own descent into dementia began at the age of 78. She showed early symptoms similar to those of her mother. She asked me if her parents were dead. She often lost things. She misplaced her spare keys to the house and claimed that, in a dream, she had seen the keys in my purse. I searched my purse in front of her to show her I did not have her keys. She set off to her bedroom to look for the keys and yelled, "I found them!" When she returned, she was holding her glasses.

She could not manage her checkbook anymore, its register littered with scratch-outs and stubs of entry pages missing because she had ripped them out. She became a danger to herself. She could not manage her medicines and confused the doses of her glaucoma drops. She would forget to eat, although I provided her plates of food.

After an unsuccessful driver's exam, she lost her license. It was a crushing blow to her, but stop signs no longer meant anything to her. She had become a hazard to other drivers. She refused to move from her home.

In the midst of caring for Mom, our family faced another tragedy. Aunt JoAnn died suddenly following a horrific car crash. She was driving home from a local store where she had bought seed for her beloved wild birds. A distracted driver lost control of her car and crashed into the driver's side of JoAnn's car. My husband, son, and I went to tell my mother about JoAnn's death. The three of us looked at one another. We could tell the news did not fully register with her.

It was midnight. A lone songbird began singing in an azalea bush filled with lavender blooms near the front door.

Our family was reeling with grief. I was devastated by the death of my beautiful, artistic aunt. As time passed, I had a comforting thought: JoAnn never realized her greatest fear— inherited dementia.

Mom had often commented that she never wanted to be a burden. She did not want to be verbally abusive to us or cause us to experience what she had endured as a caregiver. Sadly, her behavior toward us was very much like her mother's behavior, if not worse.

My sister and I made appointments with two different neurologists. Both of them believed Mom did not have dementia and insisted her condition was related to depression caused by her grief over my brother's suicide ten years earlier and by my father's death following multiple strokes.

Mom had enjoyed a successful career as head of payroll for a corporation. Her business skills enabled her to master a talent for disguising her symptoms by acting as if all were well. To her doctors, caregivers, and friends at church, she was quite different. She was the sweet little old lady who charmed everyone. To my sister and me, not so much.

Time in a Circle

We knew Mom's doctors were not asking the right questions. Eventually, the third neurologist asked the right question, "Can you draw a clock face for me?"

Mom could not do it. Time and clocks eluded her. Her clock looked like a Salvador Dali drawing.

Her memory spiraled downward for another four years.

Sometimes at breakfast now, I sketch a clock face on a paper napkin and fill in all the numbers. I do not set the clock to any specific hour. I simply need to know if I'm drawing my clock or Dali's.

I'm 74 years old, and I wonder if time is a circle. •

Carroll Taylor is a writer, poet, and playwright. She is the author of two young adult novels, *Chinaberry Summer* and *Chinaberry Summer: On the Other Side* and two children's books, *Feannag the Crow* and *Ella's Quilt*. Her poems have appeared in anthologies and online. A retired educator, Taylor is a member of NC Writers' Network-West and the Georgia Poetry Society. She and her husband live in Hiawassee, in the North Georgia mountains, where she feeds a crow family whose antics inspire her to write every day.

Riding the Memory Trail
by Landis Wade

Two weeks before we took the final, emotional step of selling our house of 30 years and transferring the deed to a couple who, we hoped, would do what we had done—turn that house into a home, we had a yard sale. That experience taught us a lesson. And, because size does matter when you downsize, we learned what we did not know about the geometry of a house.

Fair question: Can anyone really know how much stuff their house can hold until they empty it? In our defense, and in defense of everyone who has lived alongside well-hidden stuff for many years, I submit that the answer is an unmistakable "No."

"How much will you take for that?" the man asked.

"What do you think is reasonable?" I responded.

He laughed. I laughed. He didn't need the thing. I didn't want the thing. But neither of us wanted to make the first move.

We should have known that our home had long doubled as a storage facility, where each room and every closet, nook, and cranny in each room, served as individual storage units. And we should have considered the extra storage capacity in each unit. Like the spaces under the furniture, the spaces in the corners, the spaces on the shelves, the spaces behind the spaces, and, of course, the extra spaces, like the crawl space, the attic space, and the outside storage space. And we should have paid more attention to the rooms once occupied by the non-paying tenants—whom we now call our adult children— and we should have had the foresight to predict that those "deadbeats" would not reclaim anything from their storage units after they left town.

A woman older than my 65 years ran her hand along the top of a solid wood cabinet and looked my way. "I see you're selling this for $20."

"Actually, it's $25," I said. "It's the closest thing we have to an antique."

"What's the least amount you will take?" The woman looked around the carport, her hand grazing the top of the piece, trying to appear disinterested. When I cut her a deal, she smiled and clapped her hands, and when I carried the cabinet to her car, I realized that this stuff was now her stuff and how one day, after she passed on to the great yard sale in the sky, her children would hunt me down for selling it to her.

The last customers of the day arrived in a rented pick-up truck. Because I was slashing prices, the young woman, with her mother's nod of approval, excitedly talked her fiancé into buying a truck bed full of furniture and tools for their starter home, and I threw in a rug for free. At some point during this bargain-busting bonanza, the woman noticed the three cowboy hats. She giggled as she picked them up.

Sooner or later, no doubt about it, stuff adds up, and as difficult as it is to part with stuff whose only value seems to be the memories they evoke, stuff has to go. When our children were 8 and 12 years old, we made a trip to Montana, where we spent a few days on a working ranch, learning to ride horses. It was on this "Wild West" family adventure that we bought four cowboy hats, one of which was lost to time before the yard sale. We still have pictures of us posing on horses, all cowboy-like. But those hats were transactional. The kids did not take them to college, and I never wore mine to work. They sat in a corner of our playroom for the next 20 years, bereft of heads that needed them. But still, they held ten-gallon memories, and unlike the trophies, plaques, and certificates that went in the trash bin, the hats deserved a chance in the yard sale--in the free pile, of course.

When the filled-to-capacity rented pick-up truck pulled away from the curb, it was as if this newly minted urban cowboy couple had saddled up for the first of many thrilling rides together. Their pure joy at playing cowboy and cowgirl, as they did it, swept me back in time to a ranch in Montana, and happily, I thought, our cowboy hats were galloping the memory trail once again, not to be forlorn.

And then, as their truck disappeared to the west, I had a daydream. In the dream, a downsizing couple is having a yard sale 30 years in the future. Two newlyweds, greenhorns to be sure, are poking through their stuff. In the free pile, they spot three cowboy hats looking for a new place to call home.

Giddy up! •

Landis Wade writes light-hearted legal thrillers, mysteries, and essays. He is a recovering trial lawyer and host of Charlotte Readers Podcast where he has conducted more than 500 author interviews. His recent novel–Deadly Declarations–has won ten awards, including Winner in the 2022 American Fiction Awards and the National Indie Excellence Awards in the mystery categories. In 2023, he released The Write Quotes series–8 books on writing that feature inspirational and practical quotes from 500+ author interviews in 33 U.S states and five countries. His essays have appeared in five earlier anthologies by the Personal Story Publishing Project.

Celebrating Life
by Ginny Foard

"**M**y sister Libby knows what she wants for a memorial service, when her time comes," I said as I spread jam on a buttered slice of fresh Irish wheaten bread. "She wants people to come for a barbeque in her yard, at her North Carolina mountain home. There's a flat grassy spot up under the trees at the end of their gravel driveway, looking down at the valley, birds chattering, maybe even a donkey braying. She's got a list of her favorite music to play. It's even on her phone. Folk music, rock and roll. She wants people to enjoy remembering her and the things she loves."

I glanced up at my friends as I leaned back and bit into the jam and bread. They stared at me in shock. I paused, thought about what I'd said and what they might have thought they heard, and burst out laughing.

During my visit with old friends across the pond, we three had settled in for a long chat to catch up with each other's lives. Mark, Kathy, and I were spread on their comfortable sitting room chairs. We simultaneously were deep into Northern Ireland's tea and biscuits custom for sharing time together. Out the picture window, a hill full of sheep across

the road had their noses in the grass. The shadowy blue sky
threatened dampness to come, as usual.

Our conversation had crossed into the harder parts of life.
Changes that came with age made inroads for all of us.
More importantly, we talked about losses of people close to us.
We compared how we had or had not been able to talk about a
coming death. We chatted about traditions, habits, prepara-
tions, and surprises that we'd experienced. And then we came
to musing about ourselves and our own plans.

I had been thinking, *we can compare the Irish traditions
to how we colonists do this across the pond!* And so, that's why
I mentioned Libby's planned memorial service. It was
a modern example of doing remembrances in the American
South.

They had told me about Irish gatherings to celebrate the life
of those who had passed. Those gatherings expand to embrace
the larger meaning of life. People sing traditional songs, recite
poems, pray, toast the departed, recount stories and tales.
It runs late into the night since there're plenty of refreshments.
Mourners bring food and drink contributions, including a bit
of traditional whiskey to share. Guests bring flowers and
condolence cards. Some folks dance and play a few games.
The deceased is meant to be accompanied throughout the
celebration, perhaps with a rotation of attending persons.
Modern wakes might forego older customs - stopping clocks
at the hour of death, opening a window for the soul to depart
to Heaven, and covering mirrors that could be darker gateways
for a soul.

At the mention of the Irish reciting poems, I remembered an earlier visit to Northern Ireland. At my hotel breakfast, the elderly gentleman who served me asked where I was from. On hearing Tennessee, he cheerily asked, "Do you know Sam McGee?" He saw my puzzled expression. "Now Sam McGee was from Tennessee, where the cotton blooms and blows. Why he left his home in the South …," he was instantly deep into reciting with glee an adventure story told in rhythmic verses. "You've never heard 'The Cremation of Sam McGee,' by Robert Service?" I promised I'd memorize it before I saw him the next morning at breakfast.

Later on that earlier visit, I'd told Mark and Kathy about the amazing breakfast poetry.

"Oh, the Robert Service poem," Kathy nodded, "it's common pub entertainment. My Da' can recite it at the drop of a hat."

And so once again, when I'd just explained to Mark and Kathy about my sister Libby's plans, we were suddenly in that familiarly unexpected territory, where our common language had obscured our different customs.

"*Oh no.* Not that kind of barbeque!" I quickly explained when I could stop laughing after seeing Mark and Kathy's horrified faces. "Libby wants to be cremated."

Mark laughed out loud. "Thank the Lord. When you said barbeque …"

"We knew Americans did things differently …!" Kathy agreed.

Celebrating Life

We all paused to tuck into our tea and biscuits. I added more detail, "They'll mix her ashes with her dog Molly's ashes."

I'd expected to alleviate any remnants of distress. Instead, I now saw new furrows of worried tension in my friends' brows.

I jumped back into the breach. "Molly's already in ash format. She was a black lab who had a long happy life."

We were back to full-out gut-busting laughter.

"Who'd ever thought we'd be laughing so hard about this?" Mark gasped as he wiped tears from his bright red face. •

No biography provided

Gambling on Myself

by Elaine Blanchard

I vowed that, somehow eventually, I would get the ex-husband out of my life. It was 1994. I was working three jobs, and it's not that I was greedy. I just needed to pay off half of my ex-husband's gambling debts. The weight of it was enormous, and the bitterness was enough to drown my usual good humor.

Monday to Friday I worked as a registered nurse at St. Francis Hospital. I was the day-time charge nurse on the alcohol and drug treatment unit. Arriving each day at 5:45 a.m., I relieved Alma-the-night-nurse, who carried a huge black Bible into the hospital and out again as she came and went from her job. We were all sinners in Alma's mind.

On Thursday evenings I shared my story in my own group therapy. I needed help letting go of that marriage, even though I couldn't wait to be out of it. I cared too much about the opinions of others. The group therapy helped me reframe what I truly cared about.

Turns out I'd been twisted early in life, made to believe my feelings were best kept to myself. My feelings were just something for my older brothers to use in making a mockery

Gambling on Myself

of me. I was a girl. What good could come of that? The only way to be respected in my childhood home was to be a boy or a man. I had been taught to accept that girls and girly feelings don't get you anywhere but into trouble. I had learned to pretend I had no feelings. Slowly, through one Thursday night group session after another, I allowed myself to acknowledge all those lost feelings.

My second job was at St Joseph's Hospital on weekend evenings. I got paid to sit in the Intensive Care Unit waiting room, make coffee and small talk with the families and friends of patients who were struggling to hold onto their life and breath. I could go back into the unit and check on patients and then return with an update for those who sat, weary and worried. "The nurses say he is holding his own, no deterioration since the last report." That sort of thing.

Despite all the broken hearts I saw in that waiting room and in the chaplain's closet where folks got told that their loved one had not made it, I loved that job. The Catholic nuns who ran the hospital came by to check on me each evening. I felt connected and cared for.

One evening one of the sisters invited me to take my supper break with her in the cafeteria. I told Sister Elizabeth that I was paying off gambling debts, and she put her arm around me. I've never forgotten that gesture. She said, "Aren't we all?" She gave a playful grin. "Paying off some sort of gambling debt?" That notion made me feel less like a loser.

My third job was dog walking and house sitting. I had enough
work to share some of the jobs with my daughter, Jennifer.
She, too, needed extra money. Both of us had moved
to Memphis while the divorce was in process. Jennifer was
starting classes at the University of Memphis, and I was leaving
my career as a Methodist minister.

My nursing license was my best insurance against poverty and
despair. I was in the process of getting a divorce and I was
coming out of the closet as a lesbian at the same time.
The Methodists could not accept me as a pastor if I was
determined to be honest and open about my identity.

Dog walking was therapeutic for both Jennifer and me. We got
paid to love and care for furry creatures. We got paid to make
sure other people's homes were secure while they were away.
It was nice to be trusted to be kind and responsible when
no one was watching.

It took a couple of years for me to pay off all the debts
and it took even longer for me to have a decent credit rating.
A seven-year wait and a drain on my patience. It was my
mistake to marry him and yet I had married him with hope,
the hope that a heterosexual marriage would cure me
of my love and longing for women.

Along the way I have kept every receipt from paying those
debts, bundled them in stacks. Those bundles are neatly stored
in shoe boxes. And the shoe boxes, one for each year, are kept
in the attic. They are something real, evidence that what Sister

Elizabeth said is real. *We're all paying off a gambling debt, aren't we?* I had gambled on someone else before and lost. At last, I had gambled on myself and, for now at least, have won.•

Elaine Blanchard is a storyteller, writer, grandmother, and pastor. She is senior pastor at First Christian Church in Union City, Tennessee. Pilgrim Press, Cleveland, Ohio, published a collection of Elaine's Bible stories, *Help Me Remember. Memphis Magazine* published her short story, "Highway to Zion," in 2019. *Christian Century Magazine* published her essays, "Revolutions: A Bike Shop," and "One Bike at a Time" in 2010 and 2021. She has published two illustrated children's books through Archway Publishing: *Maggie Scott's Head Got Stuck* and *Honey Comb.* Elaine lives in Memphis with her wife, Anna Neal.

Stranger Danger
by Martha Rowe Vaughn

I was searching in a drawer for the money belt I use while traveling when I found my old wooden handled, hawk billed grafting knife. I had carried it for years, worn out many a pocket with it, and used it countless times for countless jobs on the tree nursery I once owned. The blade was a bit rusty, so I decided to clean it and take it with me. A glance at the clock reminded me I had little time to pack and get to the airport to catch a flight to Portland, Oregon, with my daughter. I placed it in the pouch of the suitcase instead.

Daughter Sallie had an interview at the college in Portland the next morning. We had lots of plans for the three days we were staying. After her interview we decided to drive to Crescent City, California, to the Jedediah Smith State Park to see the giant redwoods. I slipped the knife into my pocket out of habit.

We parked at the entrance and crossed the road to the office to pick up a trail guide. As we retraced our steps to the parking area where the trail head began, a man opened his car door and looked at us. Something about him warned me: he was trouble. We entered the woods, and he followed about two hundred feet behind us. I kept looking back to see where he was. I did not like his being behind us. I whispered to Sallie, "Let's stop at the bench up ahead and let him pass us." She looked at me and whispered, "You, too? He makes me uneasy. He was sitting in his car when we came in and he got out when we returned. Like he was waiting on us." She had learned from my years of teaching her to be vigilant and observant. That was time well spent.

We sat on the bench and opened the trail guide, pretending to study it. Soon he caught up with us and began talking to us. "Where are you from?" I answered politely. He was about 30 years old, six feet tall, sandy haired, and overly friendly. "Would you like to see a tree house my son and I built? I am a forest ranger here."

"No, thank you. We are here to see the big trees." I replied, never taking my eyes off of him. Sallie stood far apart from him so he couldn't grab her. She'd taken many classes in Karate and is stoutly built. If this guy thinks he has a couple of timid, frightened women, he's in for a surprise. I am slightly built, but I can sling a 50-pound bale of hay and ride rank horses.

He chatted on for a few minutes. Finally, he left and went on up the trail. We waited for a while and followed. The trail turned left. Just before we made the turn, I saw him seated on a bench beside the path. I grabbed Sallie's arm and declared, "I left my sunglasses on the bench back there." We turned around and walked back to the bench.

"I've come all this way," I whispered, "to see the redwoods and this happens. What rotten timing. If only we had gotten here sooner or later, perhaps, he wouldn't be here."

I heard him coming back along the trail. Absolute proof he was up to no good. I pulled my old hawkbill knife out of my pocket and began to clean my fingernails with it. His eyes widened when he saw the knife.

He tried to start up another conversation with us. I just looked at him with no expression on my face. I was reaching my limit of patience. He was wasting our precious time and ruining our day. Sallie moved behind him making him nervous.

"Perhaps you had best be on your way whichever way you are going," I said in the nicest Southern drawl I could muster with an underlayment of menace, coupled with a gesture of the knife.

"Uh. Yes, goodbye," he mumbled. He stepped a wide margin around me and left toward the beginning of the trail.

After visiting the huge trees—and, yes, they are magnificent but that's another story—we reported the man to the park office. They assured us that no park ranger would be building a tree house in the park and no park ranger would be off duty in the park.

Our timing was unfortunate, but our instincts were faultless. •

Stranger Danger

Martha Rowe Vaughn lives in Mount Airy, North Carolina, and is a member of a local writers group that has been meeting for over 15 years. During that time, she has published two books: *Grandma's Trunk* (non-fiction) and *Crossroads* (fiction). An interest in genealogy and family history prompted her to write both books. She graduated from The University of Kentucky with a degree in horticulture and owned and operated a tree nursery for 22 years. In retirement, she volunteers her horticulture knowledge and skill to local non-profit organizations.

Friends by Mishap
by Suzanne Cottrell

I count one trunk in the second-floor dorm room of Haus Steineck.

"Mine should be here!" my voice cracks.

My mom helped me ship my blue metal trunk well before my September 15th flight from New York City to Frankfurt and the bus ride to Mehlem, Germany. *Where is it?*

Harriett, one of my two, assigned roommates, says, "Don't worry. Our trunks…"

"This can't be happening." I smack my palm against the wardrobe.

"… are here somewhere." Her face wears a half-smile.

Harriett and I scowl while we watch Cheryl unpack her trunk.

Harriett is a political science transfer student, and Cheryl is a music education major. As a history major at East Carolina University, I was excited to explore the Roman ruins at Trier, the Cologne Cathedral, and the Louvre.

I fidget with my watch as if a solution to the problem might be minutes away. Harriett suggests we check with the administrative assistant, so we rush downstairs to the first-floor office. As Pia runs her index finger down a roster, I cross my fingers and whisper, "Please."

"Not yet," she announces.

We huff and leave. Thankfully, Harriett and I each crammed as much as we could into our flight luggage, so we can manage for a week or two, if we must. Each morning, we check. No trunks. Based on our tracking information, our trunks were on the same cargo vessel with an arrival date of September 10th, but it's now the 18th. *What if they lost our trunks?* Harriet and I lament the delay as we tug on our slacks, now getting too snug from eating a starchy diet. We miss our moms' home cooking. I battle homesickness.

I call home and rant to my mom. "I need my stuff. We're going to Paris in two weeks." My mom consoles me as best she can.

On Oct. 8th, between a lunch of bratwurst and sauerkraut and our geography class, Harriett grabs my arm. "My trunk is here!"

"Mine, too?" I ask with hope. Harriett shakes her head.

I join her in our room for her trunk's grand opening. She points at our shoes. "What size?"

"7½ B"

"Me, too," she chirps. "Try mine on."

I swallow hard and clear my throat. "Thanks, but..." I fuss when my sister borrows my clothes. Having known Harriett for only three weeks, I make excuses.

Harriet and I arrive early for our classes. We both use color-coded notebooks, and we study and practice our conversational German together. Sprawled on our beds, we read each other's family letters and nod at similarities, like having three younger siblings. If I had my trunk, I could show her photos of my family and friends. At least I can enjoy hers. In our free time, we stroll along the Rhine River, make up stories about the Drachenfels Castle ruins on the hillside dotted with vineyards, and discuss potential graduate school programs. We satisfy our sweet tooths with marzipan confections from the local bakery. Spending most of our time together, classmates call us "Chip and Dale," like the Disney chipmunk pals.

When we receive "Dear Jane" letters from home, we hug, cry, and curse. Harriett grabs her brown plaid sheath and holds it up to me. I give in and try on the dress. "Let's go." To soothe our aching hearts, we amble into town for gelato. Sitting on a stone wall, we savor our frozen treats while we rebuke our former boyfriends and rate our male classmates.

An unimaginable six weeks after my arrival, a letter comes saying my trunk arrived in Bremen and will travel the 212 miles to Bonn by train. With a sour taste in my mouth, I mumble, "By rail, good luck." The train schedules are unreliable. "Are they kidding?"

Harriet reads the letter and hands me a tissue as we commiserate. She pats my shoulder. "We'll find your trunk."

Friends by Mishap

I plead with Dr. Indorf, the program director. He recommends Pia drive me three hours to Bremen. When we arrive at the import warehouse, my jaw drops at the sight, similar to the U.S. Government warehouse in the last scene of *Raiders of the Lost Ark*. After two hours of searching, "My trunk! There!" I shout. It is battered but intact. Thank goodness. Tonight I can sleep in my floral flannel nightgown. Tomorrow I can wear my navy sweater and plaid skirt, along with my Mary Jane shoes. My homesickness starts to wane a bit.

When I return, Harriett beams. "Your trunk!" We recruit two guys to carry it to our room. When I pull out my brown leather boots and hold up my burgundy dress, Harriett's voice and mine bubble together with excitement. We plan new comingled outfits for our upcoming trip to Zermatt, Switzerland. Our new wardrobe options happily expand amidst a friendship which, during the waiting, has already blossomed. •

Suzanne Cottrell, a member of the Taste Life Twice Writers and NC Writers' Network, lives with her husband in Granville County, North Carolina. An outdoor enthusiast and retired teacher, she enjoys reading, writing, knitting, hiking, and Pilates. Her prose has appeared in numerous journals and anthologies, including the Personal Story Publishing Project, Inwood Indiana Press, Quillkeepers Press, and *Parks and Points*. She's the author of three poetry chapbooks: *Gifts of the Seasons, Autumn and Winter* ; *Gifts of the Seasons, Spring and Summer* ; and *Scarred Resilience*; and *Nature Calls Outside My Window, A Collection of Poems and Stories*.

Bad Bob

by Barbara Reese Yager

Our mother always covered up for my brother, Bob, no matter how illegal, immoral, or idiotic. Because ten years separated us, I was in my 30s before I made the connection between his need to be bad and her need to rescue him. It lasted her lifetime.

I adored him. Dark wavy hair with sky blue eyes. He was often compared to the heart throb of the day, Tom Jones. A big smile lit his face. He possessed a great personality and disarming demeanor. He was charming and persuasive. He had no shortage of women in his bed, mostly married.

By the age of 6, he had started three fires. At Dad's car dealership, he used the cigarette lighter to burn through the front seat of a customer's car. He started a fire in our home basement once and another in the school bathroom for which he was expelled. He was sent to a New York military boarding school at 7. As a teen, he was expelled for fighting. At Deveraux near Philadelphia, he might have graduated. Later, he enlisted in the Marines to stay away from Dad. At Parris Island, Bob spent so much time in the brig, he was discharged for fighting.

Bob had endless relationship problems. I recall a woman came to the house to speak with my mother. She was a nurse, married and pregnant by my brother. Peeking from my room at the age of 12, I saw Mom draw up her 5-foot 2 frame to be a fearless lioness. Her tone was low and menacing. The gal left with instructions to pass the baby off as her husband's. I was in awe of my mother's will to protect.

Patty, a sweet gal from Alabama, was his first wife. They had a baby girl. When they lived in Florida, Bob was a dance instructor with extra night activities at that studio. One night, Patty questioned what he had been doing. He tried to beat her into silence. She ran out of the house with just their baby on her hip. At a stranger's home, Patty called her parents to pick them up. None of us saw them again.

I was a witness to Mom and Bob badgering his second wife into marriage. It went on for days over dinner. Kay was not having sex before marriage. Thus, the pressure. At 15, I knew it was wrong. Once married, Bob gave her crabs from cheating, threw her over the bed miscarrying their first pregnancy, and beat her so often she called Mom for help. Mom took her to the magistrate office to swear out a restraining order. Twice. And twice the magistrate talked Kay out of it because my brother would lose his job as a city firefighter. The beatings stopped, but the cheating continued. It was a small town and my brother boasted. I knew about my high school friend, my college friend's sister, and the next-door neighbor with her new, augmented boobs. Kay moved out when Bob was on a 24-hour shift at the fire station. Mom and Bob told me off for spilling the beans. But I hadn't. My brother's girlfriends used his gas credit cards, signing their own names. Kay opened the mailed receipts. Why blame me?

When you dial 911 and say you have a bomb in your mailbox, they send the fire department. Kay, then his ex-wife, found the brown paper-wrapped box saying there was a bomb inside. When she dialed 911, my brother's coworkers came to her rescue. On the note inside, Bob threatened to cut off child support. The bomb was a hoax. That did not stop the City from demanding my brother's early retirement. He went to live as "Bad Bob" in Daytona Beach. He and his three Harleys were happy. I saw some fairness, at last.

After thirty silent years, Bob asked me to meet him for lunch. Could I? He brought Mom's charm bracelet as a peace offering. I was touched. But he had not changed. Our moral lives were not similar, but he was the only person who shared our parents. I craved them. He knew stories I had never heard. We had a peaceful five years. Christmas. Overnight stops. Picnics at our farm. Sometimes touching. Occasionally, he needed a slap-up-side-of-his-head for certain offensive words. I obliged.

Bob died of a massive cardiac arrest under the hands of an ER doctor. He would have wanted to go down in flames on his Harley. I can never forgive Mom and Bob's legacy of self-obsession; nor can that legacy change. We are all inadequate human beings, aren't we?

But I could give Bob what he wanted—to be part of a family. In five years, I gave, and I healed. I hope he did too. Our time

Bad Bob

135

together in those last years was for us both a gift welded by compassion. •

Barbara Reese Yager, or Bay, as she is known to her friends, lives on Waggin Tail Farm near Fort Mill, South Carolina. Her writing is distinguished by raw emotions reflective of deep love and shattering loss, bottomless belly laughs, and the inevitable events of life.

Her crisp style was honed writing performance poetry with the Perpendicular Poets of Charlotte, North Carolina. She is a member of the Charlotte Writers Club and Charlotte Lit. Tales of her family, friends, dogs, and horses can be found at waggintailfarm.com.

Meant To Live Forever

by Jill Amber Chafin

A t a recent appointment, a doctor I'd only seen once before grasped a framed picture of his late wife.
"It's been ten years since she passed," he murmured.

He'd mentioned this loss during a previous visit but now, reeling from my own grief, I understood the depth of his pain.

"I get it," I said. "I lost my grandmother a month ago."
She was here, I heard her voice, then she was gone—a rainbow fading into mist.

"That's not the same thing," the doctor snapped, his eyes narrowing. "Losing a grandmother is not the same as losing a spouse."

I squirmed in my seat. *Am I not allowed this grief?*
"We—we were really close," I stammered, trying to convince him to accept my sadness.

"No," he said firmly, shaking his head. "Grandmothers are meant to die."

His harsh statement swirled around the room, making me dizzy with disbelief. But aren't we all meant to die—eventually?
Meant To Live Forever

"My grandparents loved each other for 74 years," I blurted, refusing to give up.

"Oh." He slowly exhaled. "Your poor grandfather."
I studied his eyes: soft, yet hard; cold, yet warm. His grief remained lodged in his heart, refusing to budge, even after a decade of suffering.

I bowed my head in defeat. He was right. I did not know what it was like to lose a spouse—not yet. But even if a grand-parent's death is meant to be, as this doctor so bluntly put it, didn't I still have the right to mourn this loss?

I last spoke to Grandma on my birthday, six days before her passing. Her final days were spent flying to Missouri to attend her great-nephew's wedding, twirling on the dance floor as if she would live forever. I always believed she would outlive us all, just as I once believed my *Cabbage Patch* doll would come to life if I loved her hard enough.

When I got the call, I dropped everything and drove two hours to hold Grandma's hand. Ten of us crowded close, whispering memories and gratitude while machines kept Grandma's oxygen flowing, her blood pumping.

Then her heart rate dropped, and, with no real choice, the decision was made to disconnect her ventilator. We asked my grandfather if he needed some private time with Grandma first.

"I'm too upset to think about sex right now," he said, without missing a beat.

The room exploded in laughter, including the nurse, helping ease the awful truth that Barbara Ann Shaw, at 88 years old, was not immortal after all.

I succumbed to the ugly, snotty, head-pounding crying, choking on my breath as the nurse pulled the curtain closed. It took ten minutes.

My job's bereavement policy, as if in agreement with my doctor, only applied to immediate family members—not grandmothers. But this wasn't any ordinary grandmother! She wasn't a pile of bones rotting away in a nursing home, sitting around waiting to die.

This was the grandmother who sent cards to every person she loved for every single occasion—birthday, Halloween, Christmas, Valentine's Day, Easter. This was the grandmother I snuggled with on weekends, cousins piling into her bed at the crack of dawn, fighting for the spot closest to her warmth. This was the grandmother who scoured my second-hand wedding dress with vinegar and a toothbrush until it sparkled and shined, and later, on a warm August afternoon, tugged on the dress's backstraps until they were snug and secure.

This was the grandmother who sat teary-eyed in the front row as Grandpa walked me down the aisle, shepherding me into my new life.

My work sent white lilies, allowing me to file my three days off under "bereavement," while friends said most companies don't make such exceptions to the immediate family rule. But the idea of an exception left me wondering: *Who gets to decide which loved ones merit grief and for how long?*

Meant To Live Forever

If only you'd met her, I thought, you would've fallen under her spell. As Uncle Mitch said at her memorial, "She had this way of making you feel like you were her favorite." If you heard her melodious laugh and fell into her cinnamon-scented embrace, you'd get it.

I miss the grandmother who taught me how to stuff socks into shoes when packing a suitcase. Never again will family parties have a table overloaded with her homemade melt-in-your-mouth fudge, Christmas cookies with neon-green sprinkles, and those caramel popcorn balls that stuck to your teeth forever.

Never again will I meet someone who determinedly drives to three different Walgreens within an hour to claim the "buy three, get one free" coupon for tissues. How her face beamed as she unloaded the 12 boxes, reassuring Grandpa she was saving them so much money.

Maybe we're all meant to die—sooner or later. But the memory of my grandmother? That will live on forever. •

Copyright 2023, Jill Amber Chafin

Jill Amber Chafin is a personal finance writer for the LendingTree, a dance and circus arts teacher, and a mother to two wild redheads in Chapel Hill, North Carolina. She wrote her first story at age 5 and has written countless stories since then. This is Jill's fourth story with the Personal Story Publishing Project. Her novel *Shaken* has been accepted for publication with Vine Leaves Press. Follow her for book release details and upcoming writing workshops at www.jillchafin.com .

A Rip in Time
by Jo Parillo

The changes I had planned for my career this time were paying off. It was my first year in oncology pharmaceutical sales and I was on my way to California from North Carolina to attend my first national meeting where I would receive the top sales award. The company had hired me eight months before out of my successful oncology nursing career into the totally different world of oncology pharmaceuticals.

When I entered my room, I noticed the blinking message light on the phone. The message simply told me to call home.

I called home immediately; a stranger answered the phone and simply said, "Your brother is dead." In that instant, time stopped. A flood of images flashed in my head like shuffling cards, pictures of my only sibling across his 32 years from the first time I ever saw him to the last time I saw him.

I put my baby brother on the back of my red tricycle and vainly tried to peddle him around the yard. Steve later became a great fisherman, but I remembered him at just 5 years old standing on the porch holding up a big bass, grinning. His white T-shirt was pulled up showing his little round belly.

Our covered porch was a favorite place to play with our friends. Everyone who came over loved to play "house." Steve was the "dad" and he had to go to work. Sometimes he went fishing and when he came home, he brought magnolia leaves as "fish." He would say, "Honey, I'm home!" He would say "Honey" because that's how our dad addressed our mom.

The bellman bringing my luggage soon summoned all the company superiors to my room. I could not get a flight home until late that night and the silent waiting with them in my room was agonizing. At last, I was on the plane, with my face turned toward the window, lost in my thoughts as I flew home, remembering Steve.

My brother was big for his age. I took dancing lessons around age 12, which would make Steve 8 years old. Once when the other girls in my class saw him, they all thought he was "so good-looking." I just thought they were all so silly.

Steve liked to joke around a lot. I still see him wearing dad's long, white butcher coat, stained with blood. He put on some plastic gloves and a paper hat from Krispy Kreme. He walked into the den, our dad back in his blue recliner. Steve snapped his gloves and said, "I'm sorry, Mr. Gurganus, but we were not able to save your baby, and your wife died too." He then turned around and left.

I remembered Steve and his blue tick hound, Jake, who howled at the full moon and Captain, the red chow, who would do anything for Steve. The dog rode around with Steve in his white pick-up truck he called "The Great White Buffalo."

Steve was a great swimmer and built like one with a broad chest, long arms, and strong legs. He was taller than the other boys his age, so he won every race in every stroke. He was muscular all over, except the right side of his chest which never developed. He could make a muscle with his arm, but his right chest was flat.

That same deformed chest was stabbed one night. Some guys jumped him at the park. When I saw the sutures, I felt guilty. Steve had asked me to give him a ride, but I told him to walk because I had to get to work as a cashier at the Winn Dixie. I felt as guilty upon remembering that horrible story as I had at the time.

Steve was so excited to be a groomsman at my wedding, devilishly handsome in the black tuxedo with a red bow tie. He walked tall and proud, making the nicest picture we have of Steve.

Steve was happy-go-lucky and never really worried about anything. He was planning to open his own construction business. He was proud to show me his new business card. Steve was a hard worker, and smart; he could do just about anything he put his mind to do.

When I had my daughter, I named her after my brother. Steve was so excited to be an uncle he called a radio station to announce it. Her name is Stephanie.

On that homeward flight, I knew that my brother's death would change everything in my life. I did not get to see Steve one more time. I did not get time to tell my brother goodbye.

I had dreams of us growing up, each getting married, having children, and then getting our families together often. Steve's death was unexpected, a shock. It ripped a huge hole in our family. That dream ran out of time. •

Jo Parillo, of Concord, North Carolina, consults with pharmaceutical and medical device companies. She is an Oncology-certified Registered Nurse and holds an MBA. Jo's principal writing experience has been for scientific journals and magazines. In 2017, she published a faith-based, nonfiction book and workbook titled, *Have You Been Pruned?* She is currently revising both for possible re-release this year while pursuing a doctorate in Biblical Studies and Christian Counseling. During the past ten years, Jo has begun writing more for personal enjoyment. She is a member of the Charlotte Writers Club.

Bringing My Father Home

by Cindy Stonebraker Reed

People talk about how everything can change in the blink of an eye. I can pinpoint the moment in 2013 that profoundly changed the course of my life, though at the time it seemed like nothing.

My mother, father, brother, and I were living at Shaw Air Force Base in South Carolina in 1968. My father was an Air Force Pilot who had just been assigned to the 11th Tactical Reconnaissance Squadron, at Udorn Airfield in Thailand, to help support the Vietnam War. On October 28 of that year, my father left on a solo night reconnaissance mission over North Vietnam. He never returned.

As I was growing up, this fact was something our family never talked about. We did not talk about it at home, and we certainly didn't talk about it in public. Shortly after my dad went missing, my mom moved us to a little hippy town in Northern California. Half our town did not know we were at war, and the other half was totally against it. I grew up feeling alone, like nobody cared, and that my father had been forgotten.

But over the next 45 years, some interesting things happened. I met a man that had my dad's name on the POW/MIA bracelet he was wearing. A few years later, I met a man, on an airplane I was not supposed to be on, who turned out to be the air traffic controller who had given my dad permission to take off on the mission from which he did not come home. I chose not to share those surprising encounters with anyone.

In June of 2013, I started on a journey, one I had not planned to begin. I was driving from Kentucky into Tennessee, and I stopped at the interstate rest area. When I pulled off, I saw seven Rolling Thunder Motorcycle members hoisting the POW/MIA flag. No one else was there, but they reverently hoisted that flag. I sat and watched. After they finished, I walked up to them and told them that my dad was still missing in Vietnam. That was the first time in my life I'd done that—told a stranger that fact. They embraced me, which was sort of scary at a rest stop with a bunch of bikers. But they told me that I was the reason that they did what they did. For me and families like mine, these men kept this mission going. They promised that my father had not been forgotten. All my life, I had thought nobody cared.

Because of that chance meeting, they invited me to attend an event in Georgia, where I was able to meet seven other MIA children, seven other people just like me. That gathering in Georgia was the first time in my life I felt like I belonged somewhere. Just being in a room full of people who understood what it was like to go a lifetime not knowing what had happened to my father was a peace I had never experienced before.

That encounter led me to D.C. for the first time, where I got to meet more families who still had loved ones missing in action. We visited the Vietnam Memorial Wall, my first visit, and I got to see my dad's name. As the seven of us MIA daughters walked hand-in-hand, stopping at each daddy's name, I knew I was with people who completely understood what the meaning was of that name being etched in stone.

Since that day at that rest stop, my journey has continued, and the experience has deepened. I've met others like me, and I've received all my dad's military records. He now has a memorial marker at Arlington National Cemetery, and I've met three men who served with him. I've had the opportunity to sit at the table with the men and women of the Department of Defense who are still actively working on my dad's case. I found the reel-to-reel tapes my mom and dad sent back and forth, so I've been able to hear his voice, now 45 years later.

But one of the highlights of my journey so far was the honor of participating in a delegation trip to Vietnam, Cambodia, Loas, and Thailand. During this trip, we met with the Prime Ministers, Ministers of Defense, and Ministers of Security. Our purpose was to ask for continued and expanded support, the turning over of archival documents, and access to live witnesses to help bring home our unreturned veterans.

Time is of the essence now because the soil in Southeast Asia is highly acidic. It is literally eating through these remains. My dad is one of nearly 1,600 still unaccounted for service members from the Vietnam War. Now, not later, is the time to bring them home. •

Bringing My Father Home

Cindy Stonebraker Reed is a Founding Director and Board Secretary for Mission: POW-MIA, a 501(c)3 non-profit based in Virginia, founded to connect and serve the families of our nations POW/MIAs and to help end the uncertainty faced by generations of America's POW/MIA Families.

Cindy is the daughter of Lt. Col. Kenneth Stonebraker, who remains missing and unaccounted for from the Vietnam War. She has been published in several newspaper columns and magazines articles. She resides in Newland, North Carolina.

Deep in the Nooks and Crannies

by Louise Morris

S he has one or more of everything you could ever imagine needing, abundance personified, ready for a rainy day, or rainy years. No matter which room you enter, you'll find overflowing bookcases; walls covered with portraits, embroidered pieces, family memorabilia; tabletops, countertops, kitchen cabinets packed with multiples of every imaginable item.

Even refrigerators—one in the kitchen, one in the basement, and one on the side-porch, all filled with delectable foods, or certainly delectable at some point in their lifetimes. This is my sister's overly well-stocked home, after all—her nest, her safe haven.

At the end of a short, dark hallway is her sewing room. This is where you'll find her, almost any day of the week, busily working at her trusty sewing machine, the latest model, of course, with all its bells, whistles, and computer apps. She may be crafting heirloom dresses and bonnets with intricate smocking for infant baptisms or christenings. Or making dresses for her granddaughters, or patching her husband's pants, or finishing up a project for a friend or relative.

Like many other rooms in her house, this one is filled, wall to wall, floor to ceiling. Entering the doorway, one must squeeze through the narrow pathway, past the ironing board up against one wall, around the carefully arranged stacks, hoping not to knock anything out of place. For other seamstresses, it's probably a feast for the eyes, with its piles of fabric, outfits from 50+ years ago, visible from their hooks, above the shoulder-high stacks of bins.

Against another wall are several cases with tiny drawers—home for hundreds of skeins of embroidery thread, all carefully arranged by their DMC numbers, except that to reach them, you'd need a stool to lean over the towering boxes in front.

Then she has drawers filled with spools of thread, ribbons, buttons, zippers—whatever you might need for a new sewing project, all perfectly organized by color, type and function. The small corner closet is more like an after-thought, but also stuffed with reams of fabric, all color-coordinated, intricately organized, and inaccessible, except possibly for an acrobat.

Unconvinced of any excess, my sister claims not to be a hoarder, but rather a collector, a curator, a creator of beautiful things, most of which are gifted to someone special. And the rest? Well, one must always be prepared, she says. Whatever you may need, at any given time, it's probably there, somewhere, in one room or another, in one nook or another cranny, if only it can be found.

Well-meaning sister that I am, I offer ideas for consolidating, suggestions for clearing out, pleas to give some away, or, most unwelcome of all, reasons to just get rid of it.

Surprising to me, she's often willing to let me help, at least to rearrange a few things, to free up a little more room to maneuver in. On my next visit, however, I notice that other things have moved in to fill up any space we may have liberated just a few weeks ago.

I sometimes ask, as tactfully as possible, how long she thinks it will take to use up all the fabric or finish most of her projects, or read all the books lining the shelves, or eat all the food that's stored away.

Inwardly, I'm wondering how many years she may have left on this earth, being already well into her 7th decade, and, of course, I'm thinking she better get started, if for no other reason than to spare her children the task of figuring out what to do with it all once she's gone. But, in my heart, I know the answer: not now, not later, probably not ever.

Then it hits me, *is this about her, or is it really about me?*
And that consideration brings me to my own embarrassing discovery. Leaving my sister with my exquisitely well-laid-out plans of how to downsize, I return home, only to see my own closets full of mementos, tools whose purpose is a mystery, boxes of left-over or half-finished projects, so many things to do before the inevitable.

Winding down a life, letting go of the familiar, risking the unknown, is never easy, but I need to stop giving advice to others and start following my own. And, no, it's not later; that time is now!

So, I look straight into my mirror, stand as tall as my 5'3" stature will allow, and solemnly vow to let my sister off the hook; in fact, to thank her for a valuable lesson. I will let go of "the stuff" and hold onto only the things that matter: an abundance of beautiful memories, the many sister-gifts I have received, and gratitude for life's precious intangibles, however disorganized or inaccessible they may be–all kept deep in the nooks and crannies of my heart. •

Louise Morris lives in Nashville, Tennessee, and is a member of the River Writers group. As a young adult, she taught English in Japan and later in Korea, under the auspices of the United Methodist Church. Her writings include magazine articles, essays, and journaling. She also helped write and edit chapters in *More Than Witnesses, How a Small Group of Missionaries Aided Korea's Democratic Revolution*, about her experiences in Korea in the 1970s. Her most daunting writing goal is a memoir of her life's ups and downs, adventures, escapades, and general ordinariness.

This Killin' Time Is Killin' Me

by Bruce McIntyre

I'd spotted Chilly Willy a few times, off and on, after my return to the Urban Ministry Center in Charlotte, North Carolina, where I'd volunteered for years and was now working part-time, but this Wednesday, he looked different, more relaxed. His clothes were cleaner, his hair not so tangled but still in dreadlocks. I didn't know who was doing his barberin' these days, but they were better than his last. The smell was gone, along with the dirt under his fingernails. His skin was clear, but the Harley Davidson tattoo was still there, squarely in the middle of his forehead. I sat next to him in the courtyard, leaned over, and said, "Hi, Chilly. Remember me?"

After an extra-long minute, he turned to face me and replied, "Maybe, but I'm not Chilly anymore. I'm Larry Major."

It turned out the folks at Moore Place had gotten him off the streets and into a small furnished room with people around to help keep him clean and sober. He had good days and bad, of course, but like so many others, sobriety was something Larry had needed for years.

We didn't talk much that day, but later, if I saw him walking between the Urban Ministry Center and Moore Place, I'd pull

This Killin' Time Is Killin' Me

over, and we'd go to a convenience store to buy cigarettes. He'd ask the cashier for two packs of Marlboros in the crush-proof box, and I'd slide the money under the thick, bulletproof plexiglass shields some neighborhoods deal with while others do not.

I knew smoking wasn't good for him, but it's common among the addicted. One addiction is replaced by another. So, I'd rather it be a box of Marlboros than a few hydromorphone tablets washed down by glug after glug of Thunderbird.

Back in the truck, Larry lit up. I asked him to put down his window. He fumbled around until I pointed to the handle, and he cranked it down. "I remember windows like these," he said. I chuckled and said, "We all do, Larry, except my grandkids; they're still trying to figure them out."

He always buckled his seatbelt since that first time he'd told me how seatbelts were a restriction on his freedom. I'd simply said how that might have been true for Chilly, but he was Larry now.

He liked the long handle on the gear shift coming up from the floor and the short one to put the truck in four-wheel drive. He'd reach over to touch the gear shift with his tattooed fingers.

Larry told me he'd always wanted an old truck, but his wouldn't be white; it'd be red. Not a bright shiny red, but a red that looked old, like it'd been left in the sun so long it'd turned a dull orangey color, like over-ripe yams pulled out of the ground and left in the field. And how he'd keep his guitar on the seat next to him, and how he'd park down by the railroad track, put the tailgate down, and sit for a spell, strumming and singing, "This killin' time is killin' me."

"Oh, and mine'd be a Ford; what kind's this 'un?" he asked.

"It's a Ford, Larry. Can't you tell?"

"Sure, man, I knew that."

The Urban Ministry Center opened Moore Place, where Larry lived, in early 2012. They called it Housing First, and many did not understand the simple idea. The old way said to quit doing drugs and drinking alcohol, and then there could be help. It was like saying to a wood-burning stove: *give me some heat, then I'll give you some wood*, when we should have been putting the wood in all along. Having a place of his own let Larry get clean and sober, off and on, for the first time in years.

Tragically, Larry was struck by a car on a Thursday night in October. He'd been drinking and stumbled out in the street from between two parked cars. It was dark, and the driver couldn't stop. Larry, a legend, lay dead in the street.

The service was at a church on East 36th Street. Larry was 58. The sanctuary was packed. •

Charles Bruce McIntyre, or "Bruce" to those who know him, is a retired business owner and cancer survivor. He lives in Charlotte, North Carolina, and is a member of the Charlotte Center for Literary Arts and the Charlotte Writers Club. Bruce believes in storytelling and "story listening" and how it is in listening that we start to understand. He began posting his stories at www.choicesdomatter.org, a weekly blog that ran for four years. *There Are No Answers Here, Only Questions* is his first published work. Learn more at www.charlesbrucemcintyre.com.

My People: Crackers, Cow Hunters, Patriots, and Rebels

by Bob Amason

Green Amason was a rounder. Pure and simple. Born of parents who founded the first Baptist Church in their little North Georgia settlement, you'd think he would have been pious. He went to Alabama and married Malinda, the daughter of a rich planter. They had children. In 1860 Green suddenly returned to Georgia with the kids but no wife. Perhaps the wife died—people died young in those days. More likely, Malinda discovered his affair with one of his cousins, which resulted in a child. I'm betting her daddy ran him out of Alabama. I can almost hear Malinda's father saying, "Git! And take them brats with ye!"

Green left his children behind when he and his brother, Thomas, joined the Confederate Army. On July 1st, 1862, they marched with the 3rd Georgia into the teeth of the federal guns at the Battle of Malvern Hill in Virginia. Wounded three times in that engagement, Green became a disabled Confederate veteran. Green did not change his ways when it came to women. He married a wealthy widow and used her money to buy 1,700 acres of swampy farmland. I'm glad I did not get the "using women" gene from him. Green was my 2nd Great Grandfather.

I never knew much about my people, nor was I terribly interested. I was well into my 60s before I got around to learning about my family, including people like Green Amason and the Yelvingtons, crackers who got me to North Florida.

I subscribed to one of those genealogy websites. Big mistake. Well, not really, unless you count as a problem burning hundreds of frustrating hours digging around in records and swapping emails with people who know the details. In retrospect, maybe I should have honed my golf game and remained blissfully ignorant of the generations who begat me.

My Dad told me that his mother deserted him about 1925. Then his father drowned in 1933, and Dad was packed off to an orphanage after his grandfather refused to take him in. Maybe that's why my dad referred to his grandfather as "that son-of-a-bitch, Jim T____." Dad was probably more accurate than he knew because I learned that ol' Grandpa Jim was incarcerated in 1903 for deserting his family. You see a family pattern here?

I also learned some other stories—the good, the bad, and the otherwise.

The good: I discovered several lines of both sides of my family go back to early 1600s America. I learned that many ancestors came from England to Virginia and to North Carolina. Then they migrated—mostly on foot—south. I found a tenuous connection to William Barrett Travis, who, famously, died at the Alamo.

Among my ancestors are nearly a dozen Revolutionary War soldiers; at least four rode with Francis Marion, the Swamp Fox. It's hard to prove every relationship with absolute certainty, but I'm convinced. Three of these were the brothers DeLoach. Dad descended from Hardy DeLoach; my Mom descends from John DeLoach, Hardy's brother. My family tree is a bucket!

The bad: In addition to Green Amason, I discovered a great many Confederate soldiers. I'm proud that they stood up for what they thought was right, but I regret that they were wrong. One ancestor owned 12 slaves. I wish he had freed them. I am not responsible for the actions of relatives 160 years ago. I keep telling myself that. Maybe I'll believe it someday.

Mom often mentioned that she grew up on a dairy farm before her father lost it during the Great Depression. I never knew her ancestors were among the earliest Anglo-American settlers in Florida. They walked from South Carolina and Georgia, survived the Seminole Wars, and made a living by rounding up swamp cattle. I learned how 1800s Florida cow hunters lived when I visited the cracker house at the Osceola County Welcome Center in Kissimmee. My Mom's ancestors had owned that very house.

One of my Mother's ancestors, Lewis Zachariah Hogan, owned most of today's downtown Jacksonville in 1815. It was called Cow Ford then, and Hogan sold 18 acres to Isaiah D. Hart for about $75 worth of cattle. Hart founded Jacksonville on that spot. You'd think Hogan would have been rich, but he was penniless when he was killed in 1837 in a battle during the

Second Seminole War. Life turns on unexpected events, and it appears Lewis squandered his wealth.

My ancestors were hardscrabble people—hungry, poorly educated, gaunt, and tough as sinew. They walked hundreds of miles to get to new lands and conquered swamps and wiregrass to create a wild, new nation. Some were well off because of hard work. Some were slave owners. Many were patriots. A few were morally compromised; others founded churches.

They were my people, and it was time I got to know them. •

Bob Amason, Ph.D., is a retired US Air Force Lieutenant Colonel who was a college professor for 25 years. A Florida Writer's Association member, Bob writes under his pen name, Frank A. Mason. Bob's works include historical novels and modern suspense novels. Two of his Journeyman Chronicles series on the revolutionary war are Amazon.com Best Sellers. His writing has been published in two anthologies, academic journals, and books. Bob lives in Florida with his overachieving wife, a professor who is the author of a series of children's books.

Dreams and Despair

by Joel R. Stegall

Beginning and endings are never so far apart in a circle, each one leading to another.

It was not long after Ben and Catherine met before they started thinking about a future together. He was 18; she was 17. In 1856 in rural Cumberland County, North Carolina, when you found the right partner, it was expected that you would soon marry and start having babies. Benjamin Franklin Ringgold and Catherine Sessoms exchanged vows two years later and dreamed of many happy years together. Most folks had some apprehension about the possibility of war with the North, but hoped it was no more than older men talking to themselves at night after a hard day's work and a couple of shots of moonshine.

A year-and-a-half after the wedding, Ben and Catherine welcomed their first-born, William Henry. "Willie" was part of their bright vision of a large, healthy, and prosperous family. Those hopes were shattered in April 1861, when Willie was 18 months old. Confederate troops fired on Fort Sumter, suddenly changing worried concerns about war to brutal reality.

Ben, then 23 years old, believed in the Confederate cause and wanted to do his part. Despite having a baby at home, Ben was among the early volunteers. In the early fall of 1861, Private Ringgold was assigned to Company E of the North Carolina 8th Infantry Regiment.

With the confidence of those who don't know a lot, Ben was sure that after a few weeks, he'd be back home. He accepted the local conventional wisdom that Yankee boys would offer no serious resistance as they were city slickers who did not know the outdoors or how to use weapons. Southern boys were physically tough from farm work and were comfortable with rifles and shotguns, both used in hunting for game.

Assigned to a combat unit, Ben soon found the war nothing like the easy adventure he had imagined. He learned first-hand that Yankee boys did, in fact, know how to fight. The Yankees wounded Ben several times but he returned to action. In a February 1862 battle at Roanoke Island, North Carolina, they captured Ben but soon released him as part of a prisoner exchange. During lulls in the fighting, Ben might get a pass to go home for a few days. In December 1862, both sides relaxed a bit for the holiday season and Ben spent Christmas with his family.

As time came to return to his unit, Ben fretted over how to say good-bye to little Willie, now three years old. In what he thought was a loving deception, Ben took Willie to the corn field, made a play gun out of a corn stalk, and set Willie to searching for his daddy. With Willie's attention on the play gun and the game, Ben walked away through the corn. Willie never saw his daddy again.

A few months later, in battle at Morris Island, South Carolina, Ben was again wounded but he remained on active duty. Nine months after Ben's Christmas visit with his family, Catherine gave birth to their second child, another boy.

In the spring of 1864, Union Maj. Gen. Benjamin Butler was ordered to move his Army of the James to Bermuda Hundred, Virginia, between Richmond and Petersburg, and disrupt Confederate supplies moving to Richmond. In response, Confederate Gen. P.G.T. Beauregard assembled a coalition of troops to meet Butler and keep the supply lines open. Beauregard's Confederate coalition prevailed, but the cost was high—1400 casualties, Benjamin Franklin Ringgold, age 26, among them, dead. He had fought nearly three years in a war that cost more American lives than all the other U.S. wars before and since combined.

Ben left behind a distraught wife and two little boys, one he had never seen. The dream of a large and prosperous family had turned into a nightmare of despair. Catherine and the boys never completely recovered from the loss of their husband and father. Economic hardship and emotional stress plagued Catherine the rest of her life. Willie never did completely rid his mind of the grief of losing the father he was playing with in that corn field.

As the oldest male in the house, William Henry Ringgold grew up feeling an obligation to look after his mother. Even into his early adult years, he continued to live at home with her. He was 35 years old when he married Jemima Page, a 28-year-old from a farm down the road. Their first child, a little boy, died in infancy. Their one surviving child was a healthy, whip-smart girl they named Irma. The first woman in her family to go to college, she graduated at the top of her class.

Irma Ringgold, granddaughter of Benjamin Franklin Ringgold, was my mother.

Endings and beginnings are never far apart. •

In his career as professor and academic administrator, Joel Ringold Stegall wrote more than 35 journal articles, book chapters, opinion pieces and other such. None of these gained him widespread acclaim. Since retiring to Winston-Salem, North Carolina, he has written a family history tracing his ancestry back to 1735. Though documentation is elusive, he has found considerable evidence that his ancestry began even earlier. Several of his stories, often about his ancestors, have appeared in the Personal Stories Publishing Project. Joel continues to write because he likes to do so.

Life and Desk

by Emily Rosen

The latest text I received from my friend Arleen was a picture of her pristine desk. This image was in contrast to the previous photos I'd received of "important papers," newspaper clippings, candy wrappers, empty coffee cups, half-eaten bagels, single earrings, pen and pencil holders, overflowing "in" and "out" boxes, and randomly placed currency in varying denominations. Slashed-opened mail hung around various peripheries like lanterns attempting to illumninate. The rest is a mile-high pile that my need for descriptive brevity also serves your best interest.

I met Arleen in 1979 when I was co-founder of the singing telegram company, "Witty Ditty" (this is another story you will want to hear sometime) and she was publisher of an anthology of stories entitled *Women Working from Home*. She had asked me to contribute an article describing the pros and cons of running such a business, which I was happy to do. My partner and I were living and working out of Westchester County, New York, at the time and were in our 50s. (Do the math; I am now well north of 90.)

Arleen and I became good friends, and a major bond that bound us together was our mutual fantasy that owning an incredibly messy desk was some kind of spiritual sign that designated us as members of "The Creative Genius" class. Through the years we have exchanged pictures intended to prove that theory, and we have remained rigid in our conviction that chaos and creativity were sacred sisters, and we were therefore not motivated by any activity that empowered us towards "cleaning the damn thing."

And here, now, with this picture, she threw me a hand grenade as I sighted a 6-foot-long naked piece of wood. *Naked, I tell you!* Except for her ever-present desktop computer.

At the time, I complimented her with all the happy emojis I could click onto a page and neglected to bother to ask what had triggered her sudden reversal of over 50 years of diehard adherence to the "Creative Genius" aspect of our relationship. When I finally got around to the delicate question of "How come?" we were 1,500 miles distant from each other, her gloved hands deep into the soil of her garden as she picked up her iPhone and kind of spit out the quotidian truth: "*Oh! W-e-l-l,* my desk is in front of a large window now, and when the window had become practically opaque with dirt, I had to figure out a way to get to it. The desk was too heavy to move without relieving it of most of its contents – and so I just made a clean sweep of it—and *voila!!*" At the other end of the phone, I giggled while visualizing what her act of "clean sweeping" might have looked like.

That's how it happened to Arleen. But in my case, an inner voice that for years had whispered assurances to me concerning my own clean-desk-o-phobia—that, sooner or later, "it" would happen to me. Yes, *somehow* my desk would "get cleaned."

But here's the point. It has not happened, *yet*. And thus, I wait. Indeed, I wait.

But think not that my "waiting" is without effort. Each ascendance into my desk chair brings a flurry of paper piling and shuffling activity, even as I hear the strident voice of my late friend Gladys who regularly proclaimed, in admonishment of my "desk mess," "Emily! You are only entitled to touch each paper on your desk one time. After that you must either file it or dump it. And no ifs, ands, or buts."

Dear Gladys, I'm glad you can't see it now.

I wait in constant anticipation mode. *Maybe today I'll do it. To hell with "Creative Genius," and all the BS attendant to its mythology. Perhaps a clean desk will foster a cleansing of the cobwebs in my brain. Just do it.*

But here's the really-true truth of the matter. For years I have intimated in subtle statements to my family, "I can't die until I clean my desk." (*Like the choice is mine?*) Well, of course, loving family that I have, their response has always been, "In that case, forget your desk. Don't clean it."

We tend to avoid such dark conversations among my kin. I am pressed to inject the lightness of being into our dialogue, as dutifully, I do. Therein lies my conundrum.

The status quo of my desk situation thus far remains unchanged. But everybody knows that sooner or later I too will have a naked desk. •

Emily Rosen lives in Boca Raton, Florida, where for over 20 years and until her recent 95th birthday, she instructed classes in memoir writing, publishing two anthologies of stories from her classes, and the book, *Who Am I?* For two decades and until the local weekly newspaper folded in 2021, she wrote the column "Everything's Coming Up Rosen." Her travel and feature articles have appeared nationwide while her poetry languishes in the pages of a fat notebook. She has worked as a copy writer, travel writer, columnist, elementary and community college teacher, mental health counselor, and owner of the now defunct "singing telegram" company, Witty Ditty. Her long-lived history puts her at an old Philco Radio listening to FDR's "Fireside Chats." (www.emilyrosen424.com)

Eventually the Gig Is Up
by Ellen Zaroff

I was working in Italy in the heat of summer, as a bookkeeper for a hotel whose local branch was a village of grass huts with no plumbing or electricity. Its focus was on the sailboats, windsurfing, and snorkeling afforded off the Mediterranean coast.

The village was set among trees, laced with trails which led to the open-air restaurant where bees swarmed over the jars of jam at breakfast time but would move politely away if you dipped your spoon into their mass. Then they would settle back onto the golden marmalade made from local oranges or the blood-red berries picked in a town, not far away.

The huts acted as an incentive to stay outdoors, used only for sleep and changing. The hotel provided a large central latrine with one toilet and a series of faucets and showers for those who were insistent on keeping clean. In the morning the chefs who had risen early to bake the daily array of breads and pastries, commandeered the lone toilet and if one chose not to squat over the holes, which were otherwise provided, one had to wait until they were done reading their paper or contemplating their day or whatever else it was which was done behind the door which housed the sole ceramic throne.

I was not legally working there. As my stint was only a few months, the company did not bother with the requisite visas and all the Italian red tape that they came bound in. When the inspector came around, I was given a "day off" and told to disappear and blend in among the tourists, although few to no Americans were visiting and my Italian couldn't possibly pass for a local, even one with a speech impediment. I relished these days off, as we were a workforce on-call 24/7, so these days of leisure were like ice on the tongue, on a hot summer day. The rest of the staff, locals, would look on enviously as the three Americans ran free, but below the radar, on these clandestine vacation days. We did not wonder what would happen if we were found out, as it seemed a charade both sides played; the ignorant work inspector who didn't look very hard but enjoyed a hearty meal of wine and French fare, and the bosses who let their employees disappear for a day occasionally, "hiding in plain sight."

We all rolled the dice that we could play this game for just a few months.

It was an idyllic time, feet hardened with inches of callous from running barefoot along the dirt paths that wound between the huts, through the bar, past the restaurant, down to the beach and up to "the night."

"The night" was the disco, perched atop a small bluff overlooking a vast sea, where long days ended with too much drinking and dancing to tunes which had been hits three years ago, but had taken that long to reach this not-so-remote island.

"I'm So Excited," "Gloria," and "YMCA" drifted through the air and out across the waves which crashed onto boulders, far below.

But even halcyon days must draw to an end.

As summer began to close its doors and nights called for sweaters and clothing we had not the forethought to bring, payday came in the form of a wad of bills which summed up my few months' efforts. It was more than could fit in a wallet, so it was hidden in my suitcase where I thought no one would look.

As we got to customs, the agent who rifled through our bags was not being feted with a meal of wine and seafood. He looked suspiciously at my tan and my passport's entrance stamp and asked what I had been doing. I had been living my best life, dancing in the moonlight, drinking homemade Grappa. But I knew the gig—and the jig—would be up sooner or later and gulped as I laid out a story about travel around the island, visits with friends and threw in a story of meeting the local marine academy cadets on the boat ride over. He was thorough in searching and I thought of my hard-earned salary going into his pocket, but when he picked up the little pink clamshell case that held a diaphragm, he recognized it for what it was and disdainfully replaced it among my belongings. Little did he know, it held a few thousand tightly folded French francs and the diaphragm itself lay in a pocket of some sunbleached jeans.

Eventually the Gig Is Up

171

As the plane rose over the sea, I laughed at how I had escaped what seemed to be an ill-fated story. I tucked my memories behind my ear and began to plan where to go for some fine Parisian food. •

Ellen Zaroff lives in New York City and has recently published three books, *A Layered Tress*, *A Tree's Tale*, and *Once, Upon Reflection*. She runs a small foundation and travels, trying to help community projects while collecting stories and sharing stories from around the world.

Our Adventure Nearly Spoiled
by Cindy Martin

Oh, *no!* How could we have overslept? We had thirty minutes to get dressed, load our luggage into the car, and make it to the Prince Station before our train departed in less than an hour. My two younger sisters, Patty, and Ruthie, and I could not wait to be on our way to Penn Station in the heart of New York City, where our big sister Ella and her husband Harry would be anxiously awaiting our arrival. We were West Virginia girls and had never been to the big city. We were beside ourselves anticipating all the things we would get to see and do.

Daddy frantically threw our suitcases, including one large bag filled with fresh garden vegetables from our parents' garden, into the trunk of our Ford Fairlane. After hurried hugs and good-byes, we crammed ourselves into the back seat, ready for take-off.

"We'll make it," Daddy reassured us as he straightened the mountain curves, keeping his foot on the gas. But when we got there, the Amtrak's Cardinal was slowly pulling out of the station—without us!

Daddy was a Chesapeake and Ohio employee for over two

decades, so he dashed into the ticket office and had them radio
the engineer to hold up until we could board the train.
No time for tickets now. Dad made arrangements for us
to get them at the next stop.

"New York City, here we come!" we cheered excitedly.
Traveling alone by train to the Big Apple was indeed
monumental in the lives of three young siblings. I was merely
15 and in charge of Patty, 12, and Ruthie, 7.

"I am sorry, Miss," the ticket agent said at the next station.
"I cannot issue tickets without your father being present.
You will have to get off the train."

Several hours later, our distraught sister Ella called Mom from
Penn Station to let her know we were not on the train.

"They got put off the train," Mom explained, "and we could
not reach you and Harry in time to let you know." Then Mom
recounted the day's events to Ella, concluding "We'll try again
tomorrow."

The next day our adventure began again. Although we
managed to obtain boarding passes at our second try at the
Prince Train Station, we were not guaranteed a seat, so the
three of us were using our suitcases in the aisle as chairs until
seating became available. At least we were close to the water
cooler and the bathroom. "What's that smell?" Ruthie asked,
poking the suitcase I was sitting on.

Ignoring her, Patty asked, "Do you still have the map of Penn

Station? We're supposed to meet Ella and Harry at the Amtrak Lounge."

"I have it right here," I replied, patting my shoulder bag. "Finding the lounge should be a piece of cake."

In time, a kind, elderly dining car attendant passed by, checking to see if we would like to purchase food from his cart. We would have loved to buy milk and doughnuts, but it was not in our budget. We would have to make do with the peanut butter and jelly sandwiches and oatmeal cakes Mom packed for us. And the water cooler was free.

Eventually, we were seated in the coach area, and we could relax for the last leg of the trip. I had just dozed off when the conductor called out, "New York City! Now arriving at Penn Station!"

We had made it! After jostling our three suitcases plus the extra one with the gifts from garden off the train, we stood transfixed. Penn Station was a bustling palace, and we had no idea which way to go. I pulled the map out of my purse and fumbled frantically to get our bearings and to locate the Amtrak Lounge.

"I think it's this way," Patty said, motioning ahead.

"I don't think so," I said.

Ruthie tried to interject, but Patty interrupted. "Just be quiet while we're trying to find this place," she snapped.

Our Adventure Nearly Spoiled

"But …" Ruthie tried again.

"I said be quiet," Patty growled.

Frustrated but not discouraged, Ruthie simply pointed and declared, "It's right over there!"

We turned, and sure enough, the Amtrak Lounge was directly behind us.

Ella and Harry were excited to greet us and directed us toward the parking garage. Harry eyed our luggage, an eyebrow raised. "This should be interesting," he said.

When we reached the car, the reason for his hesitancy became clear. It was a Volkswagen! Defying the laws of physics, we managed to fit five people, three large suitcases, and one over-stuffed bag of ageing vegetables into one tiny car, which tilted only slightly as we traversed Route 17 North to New Jersey.

Wrinkling her nose, Ruth again asked "What *is* that smell?" •

Cindy Martin is a retired West Virginia educator who now resides with her husband, Wayne, in Mount Airy, North Carolina. She has written freelance for *West Virginia South Magazine* and *Yadkin Valley Magazine* for over 20 years. Her work has also been featured in the *Raleigh Register* and the *Mount Airy News*. Cindy is involved in the Read Aloud Program and is totally committed to furthering the love of books and the written word.

The Hunt for Ancestors

by Erika Hoffman

At some point, we get curious about our family roots. When I was a young teacher in Atlanta, Georgia, I watched that spellbinding saga, *Roots*, and it made me think. If black Americans wanted so badly to know from whence they came and who their ancestors were, and it was such a struggle to find records of their forefathers who had been brought here because of slavery, then why was I not more curious to know about my ancestors? It could not be as difficult as it was for Alex Haley, the author of *Roots*. I was 24 when I had this thought.

My widowed grandma had told me my roots harked back a long way to folks in New Jersey who lived along the Delaware River and to bakers in Philadelphia and to a fellow who lived in British Guiana whose letters she had. My maternal grandma only spoke about her British/Welsh roots and nothing about the German/Swiss ones. My paternal grandparents never spoke much about their ancestors. I knew my great grandpa had been a Prussian soldier who had gotten into a brawl with an officer and had to escape the country or be executed. So, he fled to Amsterdam, assumed another identity, and sailed to America. I knew both sides on my paternal tree were German, but that was all. I lived in this ignorance until my mid-50s.

For 30 years, I looked only forward, never backward. I had a husband, a career, four kids, houses, friends, etc.

When my widowed dad suffering from dementia moved in with us, caregiving became my routine. And when he chatted with me in the afternoons, he could not recall much about what had happened just that morning. It was forgotten. But, he did talk about his childhood, about learning German before English, about his mother insisting he go to the public school and not to a private German Lutheran school in Newark as she had done. I became more interested in his roots—my roots.

The second thing that happened is that my good friend from college took me to her DAR Meeting in Raleigh. She wanted to see if I'd join the Daughters of the American Revolution. I told her I wasn't sure I'd qualify. Only one scion of my family might have been in the U.S. before the Revolution. "Besides, I don't know whose side they were on," I said.

She answered, "All you need is one contributor to the Revolution's cause."

"Sadly, on my dad's side, I am only 3rd generation-born American. On Mom's side, her dad's folks were from Bavaria."

"That still leaves your maternal ancestors."

"That grandma's mom's dad—Swiss."

"And her dad's dad's folks?" she asked.

"Hmm..."

First, I clicked on the Mormon genealogy site, and I recognized the names of my grandma's people on her father's side. Then, I traveled back to New Jersey from North Carolina to see the graves of my grandma's forbearers. There lay my g-g-grandpa, Robert Hopkins born in 1796. I joined Ancestry.com and Genealogy .com and stayed up nights hunting for his ancestors. My search led me to Cindy's List, where I soon learned I was descended from Quakers in Philadelphia at the time of the Revolution.

This is where I became a good detective. I knew Quakers were Pacifists, but when I visited Philadelphia, I learned that Betsy Ross had been Quaker. Ergo, I looked at records for battalions for the Battle of Philadelphia. Two names of past grand dads were there! Hallelujah! But, with further research, I discovered they unfortunately never showed up to fight!

 When I told my old, demented dad that fact, he quipped, "Sounds like your mother's kin."

"Is this a dead-end?" I asked my friend the next day.

"Not necessarily. If they wouldn't fight, they might have contributed in other ways that counted."

I called the DAR organization in D.C., and an extremely helpful librarian located the tax records of a distant Robert Hopkins, a baker in Philadelphia, at the time of the Revolution who paid the military taxes to support the War effort. He was my sixth great grandpa. I was in! Persistence had paid off.

My adventure in genealogy took a year. I journeyed from total ignorance about my roots to being somewhat of an expert on our family scions. What I had once perceived as a chore was actually liberating. It was like sleuthing or *CSI*!

Eventually, we pursue our interests; we find the answers we seek; we find the path we dreamed of. It might take a while. That is OK. Sooner or later, we uncover what we're looking for. We learn who we are, where we came from, and what we want to leave behind. •

Erika Hoffman lives in Chatham County, North Carolina. She is a member of The North Carolina Writers Network, The Triangle Area Freelancers, and Carteret Writers. Her stories have been featured over 430 times in anthologies, ezines, magazines, and newspapers. For sale on Amazon are compilations of some of her published pieces. In addition, two small traditional presses published her novels. Her first, *Secrets, Lies, and Grace*, was produced by Comfort Publishing. A pseudonym was used: Riki Vogel. In 2019, Library Partners Press of Wake Forest University published her mystery, *Why Mama*.

Country Skills for City Girls

by Jennie Boulden

A s a family, we stuck close to home. My brother and I spent countless hours in our own yard, climbing trees, playing games, and working in the garden. We made short trips to visit family in the area, but nothing too far from home.

At Thanksgiving, Easter, and Christmas, our extended family of 22 always got together at my Grandma Myrtle's house in Greensboro, North Carolina, but when I was 7, it was decided that we would all make the trip her parent's home. My great-grandparents, Charles C. and Robena Poe, were aging, and it was time for my generation to know something of our heritage and their way of life, before it was too late.

Early Thanksgiving Day that year, we made our way to the Poe's home about an hour away, in the small town of Moncure, population 652, on a dirt road with no name. We came upon a rusty mailbox with the letters CC hand-painted in black on the side. It sat atop a weathered cedar stump leaning toward the road and was the only navigational marker. As we turned left at the mailbox, Dad slowed the car to a crawl as it began to sway and dip while we made our way to the top of a driveway made entirely of smooth, creek-bottom rocks of varying sizes. We parked in front of the house in grass taller than my little brother.

The two-story clapboard house stood on a rise and faced south, overlooking vast acres of pastures and furrowed fields. It was nearly as well-worn as the mailbox post, with a wide front porch, littered with a collection of rocking chairs and stools. As Mom and Dad unloaded the food we'd brought, I wandered around slowly, taking in the wild, open expanse of the farm. I had played in our woods at home, and explored Grandma Nell's place in rural Greensboro, but this was different. I saw uninterrupted nature in every direction, and it was heavenly. The adults gathered in the house to prepare our feast while my cousins and I wandered around outside. We walked down a grassy path and found a small pond and a rickety, once-red barn. As we peered inside, we saw a huge ladder leading to a loft and made secret plans to climb it after lunch.

As the day progressed, the need for a bathroom inevitably came up. The secret the grownups knew that we kids did not, was that there was no bathroom indoors, but rather an outhouse located a short distance behind the big house. Now, I'm a city girl, and even though I had witnessed a meager share of nature's rawness, I was in no way prepared for the stench of that two-holer or the facts that the toilet paper hung on a stick and the walls were lined with newspaper to insulate it. My mother had the honor of showing me the ropes, like, be sure to hold on to the sides of the hole, daughter, because you *do not* want to fall in. I was petrified that I, or something else valuable would drop in there. Also, it was at this moment, on this day, that the life lesson mother taught me about "mouth breathing," is a skill I still use today, when smells are dire.

Later that afternoon, all seven cousins were treated to our first lesson in pole fishing. Because of my outdoor know-how back home, I was appointed as the official worm threader. (I know you must envy me right about now.) We found some bamboo poles with red and white bobs at the end of short fishing lines, and we took turns casting into the shallow pond. Our skills and our catch were meager, but it was a thrilling experience, just the same. We climbed the ladder to the hay loft, where we giggled, romped, and played hide-and-seek, having a grand time until the first mouse crossed our path. We crossed hay lofts off our list; at least the girls did.

As we visited the farm in the years that followed, we saw modernization slowly touch Charlie and Robena's simple way of life. They stayed and enjoyed it as long as they could. Eventually, though, progress intervened, and their land was taken to make way for creating Jordan Lake in 1967. They moved to the city that year to live with Grandma Myrtle. Although they were well cared for there and lived several more years in her home, I sensed in them a deep longing for waving grasses and quiet, open spaces; something that clipped lawns and paved roads just could not satisfy.

The sweetness and innocence of time spent with family in that magical place in the country touched each of us deeply. Everyone should know the absolute joy of wandering amongst nature unsupervised. I highly recommend it. •

Country Skills for City Girls

Jennie Boulden lives in Greensboro, North Carolina, and is a member of the Memory Makers writing group. She has had a lifelong love of the written word. Both sides of her family have deep roots in North Carolina and have been a constant source of enriching stories.

Elephant Encounters

by Barbara Houston

"What animals would you like to see today?" our driver and tour guide asked.

"Lions," was the unanimous response from the seven people sitting in the jeep.

It was January 2001 and our first day in Kruger National Park, South Africa. Our tour guide and another passenger were sitting in the first row. My husband, Jerry, was sitting to my right in the second row and a woman was sitting on my left. The raised seat behind us held three additional tourists. The open-air jeep allowed everyone to see and photograph the magnificent African animals.

Our guide chatted on his walkie-talkie with another guide who had spotted some lions, so off we went on our search. After a short drive over a bumpy dirt road through the park, someone yelled, "There they are!" The driver stopped the jeep as all eyes focused on the road ahead. Three mangy-looking male lions ambled by us about six-feet away. The click, click, click, click of the cameras filled the air. You might think that we would be frightened, but we were not. Although we were thrilled to see the "kings of the jungle" so close, the lions obviously were not interested in us and did not even look in our direction.

After getting our wish so early in the day, we could not imagine anything more exciting. We drove through the African bush on an unpaved dusty road surrounded by dense evergreen shrubs, dried brush, dry brown grasses, and Umbrella Acacia and Flat Top Acacia trees. The guide pointed out colorful birds and small animals. Warthogs wandered around foraging for roots and grasses.

Out of nowhere, a ten-foot-tall bull elephant stepped in front of our jeep. His thunderous ear-piercing trumpeting made the hairs on my arms stand up. I gasped, terrified, as this animal walked toward our jeep with head held high and ears flaring outward. He stood in front of us, his eyes focused on the jeep. Growling and rumbling, he blocked our path as if daring us to move. I was tense and frightened facing this angry, monstrous beast, believably a descendant of prehistoric mastodons. The driver revved up the motor. The elephant backed away. The elephant came back toward the jeep. The driver revved the motor again and the elephant backed away but then came back in front of the jeep again. This game of "chicken" lasted about four minutes, but it seemed much longer. The elephant slowly stomped to his right, kicking up dust as he moved. The sounds reverberated through the jungle air as he took his large trunk and snapped a limb from a tree as effortlessly as breaking a matchstick.

I froze in my seat, petrified, not knowing what this six-ton creature might do next. I could barely breathe as the pachyderm walked to the right side of the jeep. Everyone leaned to the left. The woman sitting behind me started crying softly. Jerry leaned against me while continuously snapping pictures.

"Be quiet. Don't move," our guide whispered. This unpredictable mammal, that could easily knock our jeep over and trample us to death, ambled slowly around the jeep, his large grey trunk exploring the vehicle. As he got to the left side, everyone leaned to the right. He then walked back into the jungle as if deciding that we were not a threat. A collective sigh of relief emanated from the group.

As we drove away, the driver informed us that the elephant was in "musth" and needed to find a female to mate. Once a year adult bull elephants go through these hormonal changes. In this state, they are more antagonistic and unpredictable. They will fight for dominance over other elephants, animals, and people, often destroying anything in their paths. Their testosterone soars to sixty times its normal level, causing them to be restless, aggressive, and ready to fight.

"We were not in any danger," the guide offered with an air of reassurance to an audience needing convincing. "When threatened or anxious, elephants hold their heads high with their ears and tusks lifted, trying to make them look bigger and more intimidating. As long as the elephant's ears are out, he is not ready to charge. However, if the ears are pressed back against his head, then he is ready to charge."

Elephant Encounters

After Jerry and I arrived home and had our pictures developed (as one did in those days), we saw several pictures of the elephant with his ears out, of course. In the last two pictures, however, his ears were pressed tightly against his head.

We will never know why the elephant decided to spare us that day. Perhaps it just was not our time to die. •

Barbara Houston lives in Charlotte, North Carolina. A member of Scribblers, a memoir writing group, she writes stories about her life and family to pass on to her children and grandson. "In Bear Country," "Music Box Memories," and "Dark Water," were published in previous anthologies through the Personal Stories Publishing Project. In addition to writing, Barbara enjoys reading fiction, singing with the Charlotte Singers, spending time with family and friends, and travelling with her husband, Jerry.
Barbara says, "Being retired is the best job I ever had."

Driving Without Headlights
by Alice Osborn

I only switched on my headlights when I couldn't see the turn and by then it was too late: blue lights. I couldn't get a ticket—I had too much going on: leaving Raleigh, North Carolina, for California in a week to share my new CD about the women of the ill-fated Donner Party at the actual site where the tragedy took place in 1846-47: Truckee, California, at the base of the Eastern Sierra Nevada mountains. I took a deep breath and told the young cop I had just come from a radio show promoting my new album and he let me go. I shook my head and proclaimed that the universe meant for me to make it to California without incident.

But then the Mosquito Fire looming in nearby Placer and El Dorado counties threatened to thwart my September 17, 2022, gig at the top of Donner Summit. The Truckee couple I was staying with sent me air quality updates while I landed in San Francisco with my guitar coffined in the overhead bin. Three-and-a-half hours away and a few days shy of my much-publicized Donner Party performance with the ideal audience, I made a decision that had far-reaching consequences. It will end up breaking my family apart while making me the happiest I've ever been in my life.

Back in July before this flight, I had asked Mike of the Truckee couple if another local show could be arranged for me while I was in town. He introduced me to Norm, another retiree and a board member of the local music school. This additional gig never materialized, but Norm asked for my chord charts and mentioned that "someone" might accompany me at my big gig at Donner Summit. I was thinking a kid from the music school, perhaps. I was thinking someone who could play like a fiend on the spot without a lot of preparation. I was not thinking at all when I said, "Sure, here are my charts," without asking more questions like, "So, who is this person that's going to accompany me? Don't we need some rehearsal time?" I was now in California and again driving without headlights, this time worried about my shows, worried about the Mosquito Fire, worried that I had not practiced my songs enough.

After I returned to Raleigh from that first trip to California to my husband and kids, I divided my life into "Before Norm" and "After Norm." Have you ever met someone who makes you examine who you are on a soul level? And makes you question why you allowed your boundaries to be inappropriately crossed? Norm did that to me when he turned my solo gig into a surprise duo. He jumped my stage and I let him. I was mad at this charming widower in his late sixties. I was also mad at myself for not asking Norm reasonable questions and for allowing him to play his guitar with me when we had not rehearsed. As you might expect, the results were not perfect since he didn't know all my starts and stops and nuances, but it went all right, just not how I planned it.

I thought that would be the end of it, but I heard a voice inside my head that said, "No. Norm has something to teach you."

California. I knew I belonged there, but how could I get there from North Carolina? In the meantime, I became obsessed with the weather in Truckee, heightened by my daily texting with Norm who shared open mic videos from folks from the music school as well as weather shots from all the atmospheric rivers which eventually caused Truckee and its surroundings to experience the second snowiest winter on record. I became obsessed with Norm, more for him representing a California dream than the real person, I later reflected.

I soon found myself swaying over a canyon—highs and then the deep disappointments. I ended this strange and wonderful and toxic friendship with Norm after seven months. By then I already knew I had to return to California when the snow melted and start a band with folks he had played with from his videos.

Separately from Norm, but also because he forced me to face the truth about what I had been avoiding for years, I decided to end my marriage. It was time. My soon-to-be ex-husband supported me, which I was not expecting. I applied for a seasonal summer job at Lake Tahoe through the Sierra State Parks Foundation and soon found my way to California alone driving with my headlights on, choosing to love myself with all my flaws and quirks, with the hope that I'd find my own path somewhere along this new road. •

Driving Without Headlights

Alice Osborn is an accomplished songwriter, historian, and poet, who seizes the call of home, humor, and identity to influence her neo-folk vibe. Educated at both Virginia Tech and North Carolina State, she has published four books of poetry and is currently working on a historical novel/memoir about the Donner Party tragedy of 1846-47. Her most recent CD is *Skirts in the Snow*, her most personal album yet, incorporating the theme of love, relationships, and social class against the backdrop of the Sierra Nevada Mountains' climate concerns. Listen more at www.aliceosborn.com.

My Timely Choosing
of *War and Peace*
by Beth Bixby Davis

Never have I climbed Mount Everest and had to brave
5.5 miles above sea level in the "death zone" where
the body is starved for oxygen. Never have I skied
Rambo at Crested Butte Mountain Resort at a 55-degree pitch
for 300 yards. Never have I parachuted out of a perfectly good
airplane or run a marathon of 26.2 miles or successfully made
sour dough bread. But I have read *War and Peace*.

Leo Tolstoy's novel is widely acknowledged to be the greatest
novel ever written with its word count of 587,287 that an
average reader is supposed to finish in 38 hours and 46
minutes. Let me be clear that I am not asking for praise or
accolades from anyone; I know that many people have read
this 1273-page, critically acclaimed Russian novel with ease
and amazement.

When the opportunity arose to take an 8-week class on
War and Peace, I decided it was time to take up the challenge
of reading a book that I had long avoided.

Getting started for the first 200 pages or so was difficult.
The Russian names were long, unfamiliar, and confusing.
Everyone seemed to be a Count, Prince or Princess and were

known by different names, depending on who was discussing them. Many spoke in French which I don't read, and I would have to refer to the footnote with the English translation in a tiny two-point font. Eventually the family names of *Bezukhov, Bolkonsky, Rostov* and *Kuragin* started to sound familiar as they were woven through the story. It is said that we meet nearly 600 people in this book. I did not count, but I believe it.

Thanks to modern-day search engines, my vocabulary improved a great deal. Did you know that a *Redoubt* is a temporary fortification typically square or polygonal without flanking defenses and that a *Knout* is a whip used to inflict punishment, often causing death? Also, a *Droshky* is a low, four-wheeled open carriage and a *Britzka* is an open carriage with space for reclining. A *Boyars* is a member of the old aristocracy in Russia, next in rank to a prince. If one is named for a saint, once a year they celebrate their Name Day which is special like a birthday. I learned the differences between *Serfs, State Peasants,* and *Crown Peasants.* This list could go on forever.

I learned about the battles between France and Russia in the early 1800s. The battle of Austerlitz which France won, the bloody 10-hour battle at Borodino which was a draw, in which 90,000 souls were lost and Napoleon's fateful retreat from Moscow in 1812. The long rambling details of the chaos of war were exhausting. History, Tolstoy tells us, is what happens to us. Destiny is what we do with it.

Now that I have completed the challenge I gave myself, I must say that I came to enjoy most of *War and Peace.* A deep thinker,

Tolstoy spent many pages delving into the minds of the characters as they tried to determine the meaning of life. His writing talent in this book is the most advanced and skillful that I can recall reading. Nearly every paragraph is full of detail and imagery that go deep into this writer's own mind. Once I became more familiar with Tolstoy's style and the Russian names, the reading became easier and faster, and it made more sense. The help and insight from the two class instructors was invaluable.

I recently watched the 1956 film, *War and Peace,* starring Audrey Hepburn, Henry Fonda, and Mel Ferrer. My favorite version though, is the BBC TV mini-series from 2016. One is timeless, the other timely.

An analysis of Tchaikovsky's *1812 Overture* helped me understand how this prologue musically tells the story of Russia's defeat of Napoleon's invading French army. Listening carefully one will hear the French national anthem, Russian folk songs, hymns, chimes, and bells. This preamble is best known for the climactic volley of cannon fire and brass instruments in the finale. This dramatic composition has nothing to do with the War of 1812 between the United States and the British, although it has become a patriotic favorite in the United States especially on the Fourth of July.

Personally, I found this engrossing read to be a riveting history lesson that better helps me understand Russia today. Tolstoy shared his wisdom for troubled times in a way that makes one feel better about being alive.

I expect opinions about the book are as numerous as there are people who have read it, so I'm not afraid to voice mine. I'm very glad I read it, but also I am glad that this approximately three-month commitment is finally over. •

Beth Bixby Davis was born in Northern New York and moved to the Asheville area of North Carolina in the mid-1960's where she reared her family, raised Arabian horses, and had a 30-year career in nursing. She recently published a second book of short stories, essays and poetry, *Patchwork Collection Volume II*. Her creative nonfiction work has appeared in previous PSPP collections. Recently in a writing class through Olli at UNC-Asheville she contributed two fiction pieces, which were published in *Stories to Go*. She belongs to Talespinners Writers Group.

Immortals

by Randell Jones

Seven years ago, I realized I had in my life at the time five men who were in their 90s. I thought of them recently when I stumbled across the notion that we die twice. The first we all acknowledge, of course, but the second, in the words of Ernest Hemingway, is "the last time someone says your name." If so, well, we each do what we can.

Bill Ayers became a walking buddy in the neighborhood. He was in his mid-80s when our paths crossed in the cool of the mornings. I was 60-plus-a-few. He welcomed me, and I slowed my pace so I could listen. He was a 1952 graduate of UNC-Chapel Hill, and a cheerleader back in the day after serving two years in the Air Force in pilot training. Bill preferred the business world and made his fortune in the quarry business. He had a million stories about colleagues and competitors, the drinking and the hard partying that went on in the rock business. Didn't matter to me if it was all true or any true, he told a good story. Bill loved jazz and a good cigar. When his health failed a few months after turning 90, he called me down to his house. "Good to know you. You take care. Thanks for coming." That was my cue to leave. Bill had a line forming at the door. He knew a lot of people and he wanted to say goodbye to them all. I still miss him and his stories.

Dr. H.G. Jones was a historian's historian, the state's premier archivist, the keeper of the documents that tell us for sure what we claim to know about the past in North Carolina. For 16 years he wrote a weekly story appearing in newspapers across the state. He never missed a deadline, never got paid a dime. In 2004, with his permission, I edited together a collection of his selected stories to help keep them alive 30 years after he wrote them. The book remains in print, but it was always a labor of love for history for us both. We have the same last name, but I don't traffic in the frequent assumption that we are related beyond getting a good laugh from an audience. Dr. Jones received the North Carolina Award for Public Service in 2002, the highest civilian honor given in the Tar Heel State. He passed away in 2018 at age 94.

A third among these five fellows is a nationally prominent political hero in the state. James T. Broyhill was a U.S. Senator from North Carolina after serving in the House for 24 years. By good fortune, our paths crossed during 15 years of his third act on a heritage project of our shared passion: telling the stories of some Revolutionary War heroes in and around the western half of North Carolina. Before his passing at 95, he asked his family to have me speak at his funeral alongside his career-long chief of staff, a former state governor, and a former U.S. Senator. It was a great honor, indeed. And now I am helping his family publish the Senator's memoirs. His voice, his life of service is evident in every line he wrote.

Only weeks after giving that eulogy in February 2023, my father passed away at 98. I spoke at the family-only gathering. Dennis had outlived everyone but progeny who might have gathered solemnly two decades earlier to pay their respects. We remember Yogi Berra's amusing caution: "If you don't go to their funeral, they won't come to yours." Dad lived through the Great Depression, survived a world war with a Purple Heart, dove into the emerging technology of his day—radio and television, pursued business successfully, provided generously for a family, traveled extensively with his bride of 57 years, and tripped the light fantastic through 40 years of ballroom dancing. What a life! You did good, Dad. You did good.

The fifth remarkable fellow is still with us at 99, turning 100—*God willing*—on Pearl Harbor Day in 2023. Horace Barrett, my neighbor, was 18 when that tragedy befell America. He joined in the fight and jumped on D-Day as a paratrooper, 82nd Airborne, receiving four Purple Hearts and a Bronze Star fighting at Sainte-Mère-Église and in the Battle of the Bulge. Tall and handsome, he was detailed as a guard to escort Rita Hayworth around during her visits with troops. I saw him Sunday striding up and down his inclined driveway pushing his walker just for balance. He is one of the last of The Greatest Generation.

Say my name and I will live forever Hemingway might have hoped. I do not know the secrets of achieving eternal life, but with what meager powers I possess, I offer here some measure of immortality, speaking the names of five deserving fellows— old friends indeed.

Godspeed. •

Randell Jones is an award-winning writer about the pioneer and Revolutionary War eras and North Carolina history. During 25 years, he has written 150+ history-based guest columns for the Winston-Salem Journal. In 2017, he created the Personal Story Publishing Project and in 2019, the companion podcast, "6-minute Stories" to encourage other writers. He lives in Winston-Salem, North Carolina. Visit RandellJones.com and BecomingAmerica250.com.

Printed in the USA
CPSIA information can be obtained
at www.ICGtesting.com
BVHW030745280823
668895BV00002B/6